OUT OF THIS WORLD

Poets From The North

Edited by Luke Chapman

First published in Great Britain in 2015 by:

 Young**Writers**

Remus House
Coltsfoot Drive
Peterborough
PE2 9BF
Telephone: 01733 890066
Website: www.youngwriters.co.uk

Printed and bound in the UK by BookPrintingUK
Website: www.bookprintinguk.com

FOREWORD

Here at Young Writers our defining aim is to promote
the joys of reading and writing to children and
young adults and we are committed to nurturing the
creative talents of the next generation. By allowing
them to see their own work in print we believe their
confidence and love of creative writing will grow.

Out Of This World is our latest fantastic competition,
specifically designed to encourage the writing skills of
primary school children through the medium of poetry.
From the high quality of entries received, it is clear that
it really captured the imagination of all involved.

We are proud to present the resulting collection of
poems that we are sure will amuse and inspire.

An absorbing insight into the imagination and thoughts
of the young, we hope you will agree that this fantastic
anthology is one to delight the whole family again and again.

CONTENTS

Brough Community Primary School, Kirkby Stephen

Croft CE Primary School, Darlington

Esh Winning Primary School, Durham

St James' CE Junior School, Barrow-In-Furness

St Paul's CE Junior School, Barrow-In-Furness

THE POEMS

What Is A Swimming Competition Like?

The swimmers are lined up behind their blocks,
The people are getting ready their clocks.

The exciting words, 'Take your marks', is heard
And the swimmers take flight like an eager bird.

The gun is shot; a quick puff of smoke
Swimmers go like someone gave them a poke.

They start swimming in a steady crawl
And none of them for the first lap stall.

At the other end when they do their flip,
A swimmer slows down: the one in lane six.

They start sprinting on their remaining metres,
Their legs churning up like crazy egg beaters.

The cheering grows from all the teammates
And each one with great intensity waits.

The swimmers surge towards the end
And the times over the pool edge bend.

Soon the crowds diminish
And the swim meet now is officially finished.

Sajida Rahman (9)
Banks Lane Junior School, Stockport

Framed!

Once upon a time
A wolf committed a crime.
You all probably know that story,
It's full of fantasy and glory.
But just what happened that awful day,
It's time for the wolf to have his say.

So I wanted to make a cake,
One which I was going to bake.
Suddenly all the sugar was gone,
I just thought it was a stupid con.
So I went down the road to the house made of straw,
(The guy who lived there was obviously, quite poor).
Now that guy was a pig,
He'd taste nice with orange and fig.
'Go away you stupid wolf,' he cried,
'You'll never eat me up alive.'
'I get that you're feeling terrified.'
Suddenly I felt a great sneeze,
Apparently I had a cold as chilly as peas!
I huffed and snuffed and I sneezed the straw house down,
The pig landed head first on the dusty ground.
You know how I said I would never eat him up alive,
Well that (my friend) was a huge, gigantic lie.

So I carried on my journey up the road,
(On the way I came across a spotted toad).
The next house was made out of sticks,
People haven't you heard of bricks?
Another pig lived there, I knocked on the door and said, 'May I come in.'
'No you can't,' he said, 'I'm shaving the hairs on my chinny-chin-chin.'
But sugar, sugar is all I needed,
I went on my knees and pleaded.
Suddenly I felt a sneeze coming on and then the stick house was all gone.
The pig had landed headfirst on the soil,
But leaving it lying there wouldn't be very loyal.

I carried on my journey up the street,
(I really do need to shave my feet).
This next house was made out of bricks,
Compared to the last one, bricks are better than sticks.
I knocked on the door and said, 'Can I have some sugar?'
He replied saying, 'I'd rather put you in my cooker.'
So then I went absolutely crazy,
In came the news reporters (one was called Daisy)
So then they changed the story
And took out all its glory.
So then I was put in jail,
The lovely cake had failed,
But maybe you could loan me a cup of sugar,
Or I'll put you in my cooker.

Isabella Crilly (9)
Banks Lane Junior School, Stockport

Anger

Anger forms a big explosion,
Inside everyone.
It crushes
Every living piece of happiness.

Deafening screeches
Run out of its mouth.
Lumbering around
She seeks joyful places to ruin.

Rage runs around her,
With burning flames.
An unwelcoming chill flows in her body,
Injecting it into someone else.

Hunting for a victim,
An unexpected victim.
Clutching onto their body,
Giving them the worst feeling possible.

Grace Carrington (10)
Banks Lane Junior School, Stockport

The Big Sneeze!

One day Wolfy wanted to make a cake,
One which he was going to bake.
Not one which had icing of blood,
But one which was yummy and good.
And when all the sugar was gone,
Wolfy thought it was a con.

So he walked down the road to the house of straw,
He wondered if they had sugar galore.
Then he knocked on the door,
Sugar he thought he saw.
But then Wolfy felt a sneeze coming on
And then the house was all gone.
The pig landed headfirst in the soil,
But to leave it dying, won't be very loyal
So he had a pig for lunch,
It was a good munch.
'Yum, yum, yum,' he said,
Walking off with a smile.

Still no sugar Wolfy had
And then Wolfy started to get sad.
But then Wolfy found a house of sticks,
He thought that there would be a house of bricks.
Then he knocked on the door,
Sugar he thought he saw.
'Please can I come in?' he started.
'Not by the hair of my chinny, chin, chin!' Piggy snorted.
But then Wolfy felt a sneeze coming on
And the house was all gone.
He said it was a good snack,
Then Wolfy had a bad back.

'Can anyone get any sugar around here?' he questioned.
'Finally someone with some common sense!' he mentioned.
A house of bricks he saw,
Then he knocked on the door.
'You will never get in,' Piggy mumbled.
'You will never get past this door!' Piggy grumbled.
'I will never eat you!' Wolfy cried,

With that my friends he didn't lie.
But then Wolfy felt a sneeze coming on
And then the house just shone.
Then Wolfy was surprised,
It's like the house was paralysed.

Then the cops came and grabbed his tail,
And then they threw him back in jail!

Alex Redfern (9)
Banks Lane Junior School, Stockport

Loneliness

She hid from the crowd in horror,
Her crying shook the room.
She always feels the pain and sorrow
As she runs away from her doom.
Her silence worries all who care
Which is really not a lot.
Scared and quickly she bowed her head
To hide her cuts and scars.
She'd ask if they understood
How much it hurts inside.
But if she did,
What would change?
Nothing can fix it all.
Such a strong vibe of isolation
It's running through her every vein.
The reflection, the rejection,
Is there a more wounding pain?
She is nothing,
Nothing but a distraction.

Megan Gardiner (11)
Banks Lane Junior School, Stockport

Wolf's Side Of The Story

Now here's the truth
And here's the proof.
Wolf got involved
And had a cold.
Wolf baked a cake
But ran out of sugar to bake.
Wolf ran around to the kitchen yelping,
'I need a second helping.
I know I'll go next door,
He won't mind at all if I have more.
I need some sugar
For my grandmother!
She likes it in her tea
But never more than three!'
Wolf opened the door,
But guess what he saw?
Nothing but a pile of straw.

Grace Priestley (10)
Banks Lane Junior School, Stockport

Loneliness

Her heart crumbles in sorrow,
Eyes as wide as a cave,
Wondering if there's any tomorrow,
If there is it's another day a slave,
Her hair as blonde as the sun,
Her soul as dark as the night,
Her voice as soft as silk,
Her lips as red as a plum,
Her skin as white as milk,
But behind that ravine of darkness
Hides a subtle smile
And she will live forever
As a lonely and unhappy child.

Abbie Tattersall (10)
Banks Lane Junior School, Stockport

Snap

Fearsome music played in the back of its head,
A lump of crocodiles snapped in the back of its throat,
Secrets and lies,
Lies and secrets,
Terrifying nightmares from past to present came to haunt the victim,
Anger raised its ugly head,
As it roared its way through the dark shadows of the forest,
Thunder merged, lightning struck,
All was revealed,
Anger pounced at its prey without success,
The dim street lamps flickered its eyelashes as anger was
approaching rapidly,
The sun rose over the horizon,
As happiness overtook its life,
His mission still to succeed.

Maddison Cherry Ord (10)
Banks Lane Junior School, Stockport

Anger

Anger sat in a corner,
His heart beating fast,
Grabbing everything in sight,
Throwing it down the stairs,
Throwing it on the ground,
Watching the toys tumble down the spiral stairs,
Anger roared with exasperation,
He felt like he was going to burst just like a bottle of pop which has
been shaken,
His lungs about to explode,
His brain tearing apart piece by piece,
Anger felt like he was about to erupt like a volcano,
Anger lay in a corner,
His face turning back to white,
Anger calmed down.

Connor Murphy (10)
Banks Lane Junior School, Stockport

Grass

Grass, grass grow, grow
Where does it grow?
It grows down low.
Be the best,
Greener than the rest.
Sprouting out from the ground
You are all around.

Leo Forbes Elliott (8)
Black Combe Junior School, Millom

Nettles

Nettle, nettle as sharp as you can be.
You'll leave a scar on me.

Your sharp mark will hunt all around
And at the time you'll stay on the ground.

Find a dock leaf, put it on you
And the pain will soon be gone.

Johnathan Pryce Richard Faulkner-Davies (7)
Black Combe Junior School, Millom

Falling Leaves

Sparkly leaves on me
So come along and when you fall on him
He will fall, you'll see green leaves.
Green leaves on the branch,
You have given us a chance.

Christopha Bennett-Eley (8)
Black Combe Junior School, Millom

Griseley Bushes

The spiky bushes swish and swash
Through the day as you walk past.
They will pinch, so do not be last
As the years go by you will grow, grow, grow
As high, high, high as a tree don't you know?

Emma-Louise Heasley (7)
Black Combe Junior School, Millom

Wonderful Tree

Wonderful, wonderful beautiful tree,
When the leaves grow they keep us happy.
In the summer the lovely leaves will grow
On the beautiful trees.

Alexis Savannah Mossop
Black Combe Junior School, Millom

Colourful Leaves

Leaves, leaves sprinkle down
With all of the wonderful colours of golden brown.
The sun will sprinkle with brightness and cheer.
We will look forward to seeing you next year.

Leighton Charlie Hughes (8)
Black Combe Junior School, Millom

Green Leaves

Leaves, leaves so green and long,
So straight, big, wonderful and strong.
Roots, roots, shoot up to the sky.
Quick, quick way up high.

Shauna Cameron (8)
Black Combe Junior School, Millom

The Roots

Roots, roots, run to the sky
And strong with water makes them grow high.
Leaves, leaves pretty and colourful,
Make them strong, tall and wonderful.

Dior Smith
Black Combe Junior School, Millom

Nettles

Nettles, nettles
Twisted and sharp they are,
Your thorny twigs go back so far.

Leland Matthew Cole (8)
Black Combe Junior School, Millom

Galaxy

G reat and glorious
A mazing! *Boom! Crash!*
L uring closer to the world above me!
A liens flying across the sky, *whoosh! Crash!*
e X citing, come along and have some fun!
Y ou and me looking at the atmosphere.

Rhiannon Friberg (9)
Bothal Middle School, Ashington

The Attack

The dark, gloomy hole was approaching
'Everyone to your station. You must be marching.'
They are gathering closer,
You must be quicker.
Wallop, crash, bang,
They have landed.
The dark, destruction hole, you are surrounded.
'You must surrender or you will meet your fate.'
'We are not here to kill.'
'We want to make peace.'
'Welcome home soldiers.'

Thomas Luke (10)
Bothal Middle School, Ashington

The Deep Space

Stars. stars, oh beautiful stars,
So high up in the sky,
You light up the space
From dungeon dark to blinding light.

Meteors as fast as a sonic blast,
Aliens follow losing control of the UFO,
The alien pilot just fancied a snooze.
Boom, bang, crash!

Black hole as strong as bears
But no one dares to go near.

Joshua Fieldson (10)
Bothal Middle School, Ashington

Aliens

As I landed on the moon
I landed with a bang, crash and pop.
Light meteors soared through the moonlit sky.
I felt the other astronaut blasting off to the next planet.
Elephant, tiger, pets and animals are not with us,
It's only us aliens.
Neptune is our next stop so fasten your seat belt,
And off we blast!
Stars, comets, rockets and planets light up,
While we fly to Neptune.

Anya Jade Boon (9)
Bothal Middle School, Ashington

Alien Alliance

The booming of the UFO,
The raging rocket zipping past the store.
The alien alliance prepare for the adventure
In the deep, dark hole.

The banging of the alien feet,
Humans attacking the planet of heat,
Innocent aliens hiding under a sheet.
One alien trying to greet
The human feet.

Jack Ashurst (10)
Bothal Middle School, Ashington

Space!

M eteor at twelve o'clock
I ncoming aliens
L unar eclipse glows in the night sky
K ind, funny aliens dance
Y ellow aliens let me join the dance

W hite astronauts
A liens are having a party on Mars
Y ellow aliens stop the party and say goodbye.

Demi Horn (9)
Bothal Middle School, Ashington

Blast-Off!

It goes 10, 9, 8, 7, 6, 5, 4, 3, 2, 1 blast-off!
The ground rumbles,
Into space smoke appears before your eyes
And the rocket is gone.
Sometimes it goes boom
Because the engine has blown up!

Craig Stewart (11)
Bothal Middle School, Ashington

Rockets

R ockets roaring into space
O range balls of fire
C alm big space of darkness
K ind aliens help us on our way
E xcited astronauts
T he mission is over, time for home.

Luke James Wandless (10)
Bothal Middle School, Ashington

Space

S hooting stars shoot through the dark night sky
P luto, the smallest planet out of all the planets
A stronauts wear white suits as they bounce around the gigantic
  space
C omets as bright as the bright burning sun
E arth, the planet we all live on.

Anna Jayne Redshaw (10)
Bothal Middle School, Ashington

Take Off!

The rocket is taking off,
The engine is growing.
The rocket is going to take off,
10, 9 , 8, 7, 6, 5, 4, 3, 2, 1, 0, blast-off!
The flaming, fiery, fast, furious rocket flew into the air.
Once they got to space everybody had a party in the rocket.

Liam John Haig (10)
Bothal Middle School, Ashington

Aliens!

A stonishing aliens
L ively aliens partying all night
I n the dark of the night
E xcited aliens bounce in the galaxy
N ight leaves them so they fly to morning
S uper spaceships fly in the galaxy in morning, partying at night.

Hope Newsome (9)
Bothal Middle School, Ashington

Exciting Poem!

S uper shooting stars!
P owerful sparkling stars!
A ctive shooting aliens!
C ircling of shooting rockets!
E xcited jumping aliens!

Niamh Smith
Bothal Middle School, Ashington

Space

S parkling stars in gloomy space
P lanets big and small as far as you can see
A lot of aliens whizzing past
C ollecting moon rocks
E xcited astronauts you can go home.

Owen Convey (10)
Bothal Middle School, Ashington

Magical Space Poem

S uper magical shooting stars
P owerful glowing red sun
A magical glowing star
C omets shooting
E arth crowded with stars.

Amy Nelson (10)
Bothal Middle School, Ashington

Space!

E xplosions could kill you
A liens are fun and cute
R ockets can take you to space
T errifying earthquake
H orrific meteors approaching on Earth.

Annaliese Armstrong (9)
Bothal Middle School, Ashington

Aliens

A mazing
L uxury
I lluminate
E xciting
N asty.

Irfun Hussain (9)
Bothal Middle School, Ashington

The Stars

S hooting stars shoot past supremely fast
T winkling stars twinkle as loud as the fairies in Neverland
A s the stars sparkle bright, I look up into the sky
R umbling stars burst
S wooshing stars sparkle as bright as a red ruby.

Shay Noble
Bothal Middle School, Ashington

Out Of Their Mind

Aliens on Mars munching party food.
It's party time!
Pop go the wacky aliens after too
many cakes.

Corey Jackson (10)
Bothal Middle School, Ashington

Launching Rocket

The rocket was launching,
10, 9, 8, 7, 6, 5, 4, 3, 2, 1, blast-off!
There's smoke, fire
Then zooms away with a sizzle and *bang!*

Lewis Robertson (11)
Bothal Middle School, Ashington

Silver Shooting Star

Silvery shooting star! Wish! *Whoosh!*
Zooming past the bright blinding sun
With nothing else to be seen.

Ellie Fairclough (10)
Bothal Middle School, Ashington

Summer

Summer is a great time to get out and play.
The sun shines very brightly outside.
Summer is a great time to have a picnic.
You can get time to relax and enjoy the sun.
That's why I love summer so much.

Arianne Jones
Bow Durham School, Durham

In Spring

S pring flowers pop up, early on the first spring morning
P layful lambs spring about on bouncy legs
R oaring of a tractor carrying sheep about to be sheared
I n spring there are wonderful blue skies and puffy white clouds
with a gleaming, shining bright sun
N ature choosing bright, flashy and cool colours which stand out
G orgeous, distinctive flowers.

That's why I love spring.
Which season do you like and why?

Eleanor Lamb
Bow Durham School, Durham

Benjey Doggy Days

Benjey wakes up
Eats
Plays fetch
Has a biscuit
And sleeps.

Benjey stretches
Eats
Sits on the rug
And rests.

Benjey rises
Eats
Walks
Has a bone
And snoozes.

Benjey wags his tail
Eats
Goes to the beach
Goes in the sea
Returns
And sleeps.

Benjey scratches
Eats
Finds a cat, chases it
Watches 'Who let the dogs out?'
Looks out of the window
And sleeps.

Sebastian Collins (9)
Bow Durham School, Durham

A Winter Wonderland

Winter sprung
Through leaf and tree
Sunset going daintily
Through the branches
Here and there
It keeps prowling everywhere.

Winter leapt
Through sand and sea
But if you listen closely
You will hear with your ear
Something whistling through the sparkling sea.

Winter raced
Through river and stream
White new snow, it looked like cream
Don't ask me why
But if you spy
On the frozen stream
You might just hear winter scream.

Winter dodged
Through city white
Lots of people in the light
Humans spending winter warm
While poor animals have to mourn
Creamy, white, crystal snow
Very soon it's time to go.

Thea Charlotte Sørensen (10)
Bow Durham School, Durham

Congratulations your poem has been chosen as the best in this book!

Dashing Dolphins

Dappling dolphins
With their silky skin
Their joyful heart
Can more be desired?

Leaping dolphins
Feel the air
Hear screeching birds
See bright blue sky
Can more be desired?

Imbecile fishermen
Swooping nets
Hurt and injure
Our ocean pets.

Dazzling dolphins
A breathtaking scent
Shimmering eyes
A splashing tale
Can more be desired?

Friendly fish jumping free
Having fun in sea
Dancing dolphins so happy
I wish they would play with me.

Libby Nicholson (9)
Bow Durham School, Durham

Frosty Days

Frost whispers in the silent village,
Snow drops
Gently on the ground.

Snow arrives
Covering the rushing town,
All covered in snow,
Blocked cars,
Robins sing through the frosty trees.

The silent sea
On the freezing sand,
Gushing waves
On the clashing shells.

The frozen lake,
Through the icy snow,
Underneath the ice
It's what nobody knows.

Frost creeps
Through the snowy wood,
To the rustling trees,
Snow falls,
Frost is seen.

Olivia Nicholson (9)
Bow Durham School, Durham

Animals And Sea Creatures

A mazing animals filling the landscape
N ature fills everywhere on Earth
I magine a world with beauty falling
M assive lands fill the Earth
A nimals running across the land
L and where no one has been
S corching animals going over land.

Luca Regan-Teasdale (7)
Bow Durham School, Durham

The Butter And Cup Meadow

In the mist of the silvery cups
And the golden light of the butter
There lies a rather unusual man.
He lay there for two years and five days
Trying to find out something

In this land there were fluorescent rainbows
And lovely flowers spreading everywhere.
With cute little cottages, sweet juicy pears.
Buzz . . . Buzz the bees say,
Listen to the trees swish this way and that
Like the wings of an ecstatic bat.

The man still lay . . . then he got it,
'I know now,' he said,
'I'll call this the Buttercup Meadow.'

Then the flowers gleamed brightly as he said that word.
'Welcome old friend, you now have returned.'
Then the cups and the butter waddled along
Singing a beautiful, sweet, silly song.
'Since you have given us a name we will give one to you.
We will now call you a leprechaun.
Thank you, thank you, thank you.'

Hannah Mary Gordon (9)
Bow Durham School, Durham

The Mysterious Grotto

Behind the sparkling waterfall lies
A mysterious grotto hidden from eyes.
In dark, damp corners the mushrooms glow
And other magical flowers grow.
Water nymphs dance as twilight falls,
Their shadows dancing across the walls.
Water tinkling, crickets chirping, reeds rustling like a magical choir.
Tree branches breaking in the crackling fire.

Isabelle Metcalfe (8)
Bow Durham School, Durham

Rainbow Spectacular Scheme

The sky is the home for rainbows,
With the frothy, white, delightful clouds.
The rainbows are always happy,
In the blue, mysterious sky.

The wonderful colours of the rainbow are called:
Red,
Orange,
Yellow
Green,
Blue,
Indigo
and Violet.

Red is hot-headed with a lot of temper,
Orange is sweet so they look good enough to eat.
Yellow is happy, it cheers people up.
Green is delicate, it waves in the sky.
Blue is like a waterfall swishing through the clouds.
Indigo is with the sunset all the time,
Violet is always shy, hiding in the frothy white clouds in the dark blue
sky.
This is the home for rainbows where they live in perfect harmony.

Hannah Macnaughton-Jones (9)
Bow Durham School, Durham

Sandy Cove Shipwreck

Under sandy cove shipwreck
Is forbidden for flyers in high tide
But in low tide they swim with pride,
Tide and excellence.

Under sandy cove shipwreck
No man has ever been
It is as deep as Beamish Mine
So nobody can see the ruby-red sergeant.

Timon Basu (8)
Bow Durham School, Durham

The Magical Waterfall

In the Land of Magic
I strolled through the woods.
The day was fine and sunny,
I saw lots of bunnies.

I came across a passageway
And I slid through it.
To my surprise it led to a waterfall,
I gasped in delight.

When I drank from the waterfall
I shrank down in size.
I saw a mouse hole
And crawled inside.

To my amazement
It led to a garden
Full of candy flowers
And sugar pumpkins.

I returned through the hole,
Drank the water again,
I grew back to normal
And never went there again!

Niamh Gould (8)
Bow Durham School, Durham

The Bee-Jive

Buzz, buzz, buzz, the bees fly around
High, high, high, way above the ground
Busy, busy, busy making liquid gold
Honey, honey, honey ready to be sold.

Yum, yum, yum lovely in my tum
Sweet, sweet, sweet, gorgeous for a treat
Bread, bread, bread is perfect it is said
With honey, honey, honey, *buzz, buzz, buzz.*

Harriet Anne Reynolds (8)
Bow Durham School, Durham

Snowstorm

Snow, snow, snow
Sweet, loving and shy,
Light velvet white
That strokes us as we wander
Through the enchanted world.

Snow, snow, snow
Strength she gathers
Snowmen and forts,
She starts to summon.

Snow, snow, snow
Blinding our view,
Gloomy and bitter,
For some reason she's violent
I have no idea why,
Maybe because
She's no longer shy?

Snow, snow, snow
There's nothing left,
Just the glowing white dusk
She left behind . . .

Max Orr (10)
Bow Durham School, Durham

Waterfall

We heard the waterfall
Before we saw it.

Shhhh! went the deafening roar,
White water plunged over the grey cliff
While we watched the waterfall in awe.

Snow was tipping into the freezing pool,
The frothing water was bubbly.

We got in a boat and went down the river.

Robbie McLaughlin (8)
Bow Durham School, Durham

Snow Leopard

Snow leopard hunt,
Snow leopard watch,
Snow leopard hunted,
Snow leopard gone . . .

Snow leopard spy;
Your prey tick-tock
To your brilliant plan.

Snow leopard silent still . . .
With fur so beautiful.
How on Earth,
Could people steal it?

Snow leopard pounces on the human
That stole your fur so beautiful.
Don't let them do what they do.
They shall die!

Snow leopard hunt,
Snow leopard watch,
Human hunted,
Human gone . . .

Lucy Beeby (9)
Bow Durham School, Durham

I'm Off School

Getting off school with a broken arm,
Who knew a hockey stick could cause so much harm?

No reading or maths or arts and crafts.
No games or swimming, no geography,
Just watching TV and missing RE!

So boring it can be.
Who wants to be me?
Playing is so cool,
I definitely miss school.

Madeleine Yuill (8)
Bow Durham School, Durham

My Cat Charlie

My cat Charlie
Sleeps on the mat,
Or on the window ledge,
But not too close to the edge.

My cat Charlie
He's a fast mover,
When he hears the hoover.
He couldn't get away any sooner
If he ran as fast as a puma.

My cat Charlie
Is cosy and cuddly
And naughty but nice
When he's playing with mice.

My cat Charlie
With teeth as sharp as razors
And claws like pearly pins, he likes to pad my knee
And snuggle into me.
I love my cat Charlie
I think he loves me too.

John-Dylan Walker (9)
Bow Durham School, Durham

The Poem

Its colour is as white as a snow leopard.
The feel of it is like a cold wall.
It can be see-through like a piece of glass.
It blocks your doors and windows with coldness.
On lakes there are thick sheets of it.
People shiver because of the coldness of it.
It gives you frostbite and colds.
It gets you when you least expect it!
It requires many muscles to cut.
It lasts longer than fresh snow . . .

Harry Spooner (11)
Bow Durham School, Durham

My Day

I am a toothbrush,
I am bristly,
I am proud,
I am full of myself every day,
But there is one time I hate.

She picks me up,
Tosses me about
And never says sorry!

She slaps on some slop,
Covers me in water,
Plunges me into a grotto
For around two minutes.
Extracts me,
Slaps on some additional water
And leaves me.

Alone,
Again,
Stranded . . .

Charlotte Holmes (10)
Bow Durham School, Durham

Costumes In A Fancy Dress Shop

You see some costumes glittery white
Comfy and cute, some give you a fright
Some are freaky, some are cool
Some are silly, you look like a fool
Some are smelly, some are big
Some furry, some have wigs
Some have jewellery
Some have glitter
Some have beads
And that is what they have in a fancy dress shop.

Jasmine Johnson
Bow Durham School, Durham

Winegum Packet

In my cupboard,
In my house,
Sits the packet,
As it sings its song.

'Eat us, eat us, we are very nice.'
I reply, 'Is there any spice?'
'Eat us, eat us we have red,
Eat us, eat us we have blue.'
(A blue colour is awfully new.)

'We know you like us,
We know you like black.'
If I take black,
On my teeth will be plaque.

'Have us, have us
We don't contain any nut.'
No, no, no,
I'll just have chocolate.

Joe Winetroube (10)
Bow Durham School, Durham

In My Box

I have a box.
I will put a snowman in summer in my box.
I will fly in the sky in my box,
From Ireland to the USA in my box.
I can make people from the dead come back to life. RIP.
I can be whatever I want in my box.
I can fight zombies in my imaginary world.
I can make people live forever in my box.
I can fly like a bird in the sky.
I'm rich in my box.
I can go back in time.
I can make people poor.

Henrik Thomas Sørensen (7)
Bow Durham School, Durham

What Kind Are You?

Are you one of those tall people
Or one of those small people?

Are you one of those adventurous people
Who make us laugh?
Telling jokes and silly stories.
Or you might just be a clown!
You might even make people frown!

There are all types of people,
Disabled people,
Olympic people,
Paralympic people,
Black people
And white people,
Mad people
And calm people.

There are all types of people,
But at the end of the day we're all worth the same.

Alex Mitchelson (11)
Bow Durham School, Durham

Under The Blue Ocean

U nder the blue ocean
N ice and friendly mermaids and mermen
D eep depths down the seabed
E xcellent fun, swimming up and down
R acing fast on their seahorses, one, two, three, go

T he pretty look of pearls
H orrible oil ruining the ocean
E vil nasty sirens

S eaweed so delicious and crunchy
E lectric eels stinging sweet fish
A wesome adventures under the sea.

Kaelyn Jones
Bow Durham School, Durham

Toy Box Of Terror

I am scared of toys,
When I see them I make lots of noise.
I open my toy box
(Which is covered in socks).
A teddy bear rises
Talk about surprises!
A doll shakes
Like a series of earthquakes.
The bouncy ball likes to bounce
And hits me with a little pounce
Lego builds by itself
Showing off all its health.
A rubber duck squeaks again
Saying, 'Write this down if you've got a pen.'
Then when my eyes could see no more,
My box is filled with sweets galore.
I don't know what came over me
Maybe it's just imagery!

Samuel David Gordon (10)
Bow Durham School, Durham

The Computer

I wake up and go to the computer.
I switch him on and he buzzes for a few minutes
And comes up with a screen saying:
'An error has occurred
Please try again'.
I then get annoyed at him and he says,
'If you are having trouble the suggestions are listed below.'

Five hours later . . . I fix him to get onto Facebook.
He says that I have received five messages.
I then read and each of them say:
'An error has occurred'.
I give up!

Harry Cameron (11)
Bow Durham School, Durham

Friendly Friends

Friendly fun friends oh ho.
My friends are friendly.
My friends are fun.
Awesome, amazing friends oh ho.
My friends are awesome.
My friends are amazing.
Great good friends oh ho.
My friends are great.
My friends are good.
Fantastic fabulous friends oh ho.
My friends are fantastic.
My friends are fabulous.
Excellent epic friends oh ho.
My friends are excellent.
My friends are epic.
Super spectacular friends oh ho.
My friends are super.
My friends are spectacular.

Anna Beresford
Bow Durham School, Durham

The Magical Car

Oh magic car,
Oh magic car,
How high can you fly up in the sky?
You sound like a raging rocket as you pass by.

You are red like an angry volcano,
You are as fast as lightning.
You look so sleek and smooth
With red-hot burning tyres
And flashing white lights.
Oh magic car
I wish that I could drive you!

Myles O'Brien (8)
Bow Durham School, Durham

The Magic Box

(Based On 'The Magic Box' By Kit Wright)

In my magic box I will put . . .
The raging sea,
A white pony,
The dragon's deep fiery breath.

In my magic box I will put . . .
A shooting star,
A little lamb
And a tweeting bird.

In my magic box I will put . . .
The colourful rainbow,
The golden sun,
The cloudy sky,
The misty moon and stars above.

My magic box looks like it has got stars,
It has blue waves like the sea and a golden lake.

Milly Rochester
Bow Durham School, Durham

The Toothbrush

All I can hear is *buzz, buzz, buzzy.*
Please be quiet, my brain is going all fuzzy!
'Brush your teeth, I like the taste,'
Make haste, make haste!

Why is it every day that your long, thin body lies upon the sink?
'While your big eyes blink!'
Shut up you're so stupid!
'Well, you're the opposite to Cupid!'

Shut up I hate you!
'Your teeth are waiting in a long queue!'
'Those teeth are mine!'
OK fine!

Kristian Wood (10)
Bow Durham School, Durham

My Cat

My little kitty Charlie
Has little cute white paws,
But don't be fooled he's vicious,
When he scratches with his claws.

His fur is black and fluffy,
He looks so soft and round,
He loves to sleep upon my bed
And makes a purring sound.

Charlie doesn't like the rain,
He runs back to the house
And sometimes in the morning
He brings me back a mouse.

My little kitty Charlie
Is nice and soft to touch,
My little kitty Charlie
I love him so, so much.

Ella Stephenson (9)
Bow Durham School, Durham

The Shipwreck

In the deep, dark ocean
A shipwreck lies,
Fish exploring day and night
And they will give you a big, bad fright.

In the deep, dark ocean
The vicious eel and the swift shark
Linger around in the dark!
Both protecting their possessions day and night.

In the deep, dark ocean
The dead coral lies there,
Not a sound can be heard
In the ocean.

Madeleine Holmes (8)
Bow Durham School, Durham

My Tie

My tie is a sneaky snake,
I wish it would just stay still,
I tie it, it strangles me,
I take it off, it slithers away,
What will my tie turn into next?

My tie is a human tamer,
I wish it wouldn't whip me,
It even tied my hands in a knot,
It took me an hour to get untangled,
It blindfolded me and it pushed me down the stairs,
What will my tie turn into next?

My tie even dressed up as a person,
Gosh, was that day funny!
My tie once thought I was a dog
And took me for a walk,
What will my tie turn into next?

Asia Koltai-Newton (10)
Bow Durham School, Durham

Dragon's Cave

In the dark, desolate dragon's cave
A strong, powerful knight entered, oh so brave!
To slay the frightful, fanged beast.
The heroic champion appeared from the east.

The fearless knight moves silently between shadows dark,
Quietly stalking his intended mark,
A growling, groaning sound catches his ear,
But he boldly continues to move forward without any fear!

A slithering, scaly tail catches his eye
He raises his shining, sharp sword and yells a battle-cry.
He strikes the menacing, mighty dragon to the ground.
It is totally defeated, not making a sound.

Adam Chin (9)
Bow Durham School, Durham

Butterflies About Butterfly

Sleepless night, too nervous to dream.
Get up in the dark, headlights beam.
Snacks in the car, can't get too full,
Focusing on the shimmering pool.

On goes my super-suit, *snap* goes my goggles.
So many coloured hats, no coloured woggles.
Warm-up over, nerves are settling,
Over the splashes, I hear my name called for marshalling.
Behind the blocks, I start mobilising.
I step up on the blocks, ready for diving.
1, 2, 3, 4 whistles go!
Pull, pull, kick, kick, wriggle, wriggle, flow.

I thump the time board. Stop the clock.
My time is a personal best. What a shock!
Coach gives me a high five.
The pool is as still as when we arrived.

Rachel Mackenney (9)
Bow Durham School, Durham

Dipping, Diving, Dolphin

I know a dolphin
Who likes to dip and dive
He's five, I think, but we can't be sure
He's a very strange dolphin, he has suncream on his head,
The reason for this, he is such a man
Looking for danger, head in the sun
He's perfect at playing,
Jumps really high,
Then flips very well,
Excellent landing to end the display.

Gabriel Somerville-Smith (10)
Bow Durham School, Durham

Rainbow Meadow

While walking through a meadow I saw a colourful waterfall,
I wondered what it was called,
I know, a rain ball,
No, a rainfall,
I've got it, a rainbow.

The magical rainbow is so cool,
It makes me feel like I rule,
Next to the waterfall there is a pool,
It sparkles like a precious jewel,
With rainbow horses galloping around.

The enchanted horses jump and run,
They glisten in the sun,
Their golden hooves sound like a drum,
I know they are having fun,
All day long.

Isabelle Ford (8)
Bow Durham School, Durham

All About Minecraft

The growling of the zombies as night-time falls
And it's all in Minecraft.
But the zombies burn through the day
And it's all in Minecraft.

The snorting of a pig
And it's all in Minecraft.
The mooing of the cow as the day runs by
And it's all in Minecraft.

The hissing of the creeper getting ready to explode!
And it's all in Minecraft.
The beautiful sight of daytime's crack
And it's all in Minecraft.

I love it of course.

George Fishwick (7)
Bow Durham School, Durham

The Shark

The shark's skin was tougher
Than bark.
His sharp, pointed teeth
Like needles.

The shark's fin was as tough
As old boots.
He glides quietly
Through the shallow water.
Just hoping, just hoping to get you.

The shark was braver
Than a crocodile.
As he'll quickly move
To the scent of your blood,
When he'll dreadfully, deliciously
Eat you!

Rebecca May Willis (9)
Bow Durham School, Durham

The Journey

I stand on the edge on my boat
And let the crystal clear water caress my hand
As above me the sails flap like butterflies
So I lift my head toward the blue skies.

We are gliding towards a forgotten village,
White, like it's covered in snow,
But abandoned.
Where the people went nobody knows.

We dropped our anchor to spend the night.
Then as darkness fell
I lay on the deck,
While the stars shone bright
Like diamonds in the sky.

Libby Monk (9)
Bow Durham School, Durham

At The Beach

The shimmering sand and the sparkling sea
Are always there and gleam at me.
The boats on the silky sea, turn around
And nod at me.
Wet green seaweed lay on the sand.
Children use them strand by strand.
These are some of the reasons why I love the beach.

Waggy tailed dogs catch sticks.
Children have ice creams with big licks.
Dazzling shells, their story tells
Of waves that ring ships' bells.

Sticky suncream, kites flying high,
With the seagulls in the beautiful blue sky.
I find a crab in the rock pool,
That's why the beach is extremely cool!

Ella Purvis (8)
Bow Durham School, Durham

My Bed

When my eyes crawl open
In the morning,
My mattress moans and groans
And tries to keep me in place.
My pillows try to contain me
And my duvet tries to pin me down
But I shake them off.

They wail and whine as I get up,
All I hear is their sobs,
My bed tries to calm them down,
But they will only stop if I return.

At breakfast I can still hear them,
Screaming for me to return.

Alexander Cooper (10)
Bow Durham School, Durham

Autumn

Autumn moves very slowly,
In the woods it never gets lonely,
It smashes through the brown leaves,
Falling from the oak trees.

Autumn moves very slowly,
Its wind makes the sand do roly-polies,
It makes the see-saws go up and down,
Then settles on the cold hard ground.

Autumn moves very slowly,
Making the church look even more holy.
Soon autumn will be changing into winter,
The season of dark and coldness.

And now autumn is dying down,
Dying from its oldness.

Charlie Ward (10)
Bow Durham School, Durham

My Pillow

'Get off! Get off!' my pillow cries,
'I don't want you here anymore.'
(Its cover is all wet and sore from last night's shower.)
'You don't care about me
You have the power to make me weep.
You just don't care.
Every night you squish me
You never ever say sorry for what you do.
I don't like you.
I hope I move to another room
But you won't defeat me.
Every time you leave me in a dark room
With nothing but your bed,
You always rest your heavy head.
I hate you.'

Amy Moyes-Reeder (11)
Bow Durham School, Durham

The Storm

It all started with a drizzle
Like honey from a spoon.
But suddenly the water pours down
Like a herd of stampeding bulls!
The thunder roars like a furious lion!
The lightning flashes as bright as the burning sun!

The people run round like crazy bees,
Chaos in the street
Like a crazy mad scientist,
Dark clouds as far as the eye can see.

All falls silent as the storm dies down
As suddenly as it started,
All is fine now,
Peace and quite everywhere!

Chris Fordyce (10)
Bow Durham School, Durham

Ultimate Box

When I wake up in the morning
On a week day
My Xbox sits and stares saying,
Please, don't go down the stairs!
It sits patiently waiting
For five full days
Wishing and wishing to be turned on.

Finally, after five days of waiting
I wake up to a sleeping Xbox
And I turn it on and it wakes up with joy
And automatically turns on FIFA.

But sadly, after two days of happiness,
It must go back to its weekly routine
Forever and ever.

Harry Hughes (10)
Bow Durham School, Durham

Ralph The Dog

I have a dog called Ralph who's four,
He sleeps on a bed rather than the floor,
Always chasing squirrels everywhere.
He eats yummy, scrummy doggy food,
He's always so cute and cuddly, wags his tail rapidly.

Once he brought a smelly, dead rat back.
When I come back from school he is always on the bed,
Always barks and always wags his tail at other dogs,
And when he sits on your lap, he always licks you on the face.

Jonathan Bracken (9)
Bow Durham School, Durham

The Cool Moon

I aim for the moon but I land on the stars.
All the stars glittering in my eyes.
Now that I'm on the moon I don't want to go down.
Smiling and laughing someone is dancing on the moon.
Oh no I have fallen off the moon.

Isabella Moyes
Bow Durham School, Durham

Outer Space

Outer space, there are things you have never seen.
Under and outer space is very cool.
The asteroids are running everywhere.
Enter outer space and see what it is like.
Roaring asteroids making craters.
Swirling black holes smashing everything.
Mega galaxies.
Absolutely awesome exploding stars.
Moon with all its craters.

Sohan Mussunoor
Bow Durham School, Durham

The Graveyard

The graveyard was full of smoke
As the dead rose from their graves
It really was no joke
As the dead people were like slaves
They drifted through the misty woods
To come to the haunted hotel
With skeleton faces
Inside their hoods
To no more go back to Hell.

Ruby Ward (8)
Bow Durham School, Durham

Minecraft

M ining in the middle of a cave with a diamond pickaxe.

I nside my home I have a diamond comb.

N urture the grass with a spring running by.

E choing caves as the zombies groan.

C racking stone as creepers explode.

R attlesnakes that are coming closer.

A ttacking skeletons with a bow and arrow.

F ighting Endermen as you look in their eyes.

T orches glow with a glittery glow.

Andrew Collins
Bow Durham School, Durham

Monsters, Monsters In My Street

Monsters, monsters in my street
Creeping, crawling down my lane.
Monsters, monsters in my house
Creeping everywhere!
Monsters, monsters in my room
Scratching on my sheets.
Monsters, monsters in my bed
Creeping silently, they're on my head!

Innes Fordyce (7)
Bow Durham School, Durham

In Space Lots Of Things Can Happen

You might find a luminous yellow spaceship brighter than the sun
And inside the spaceship there might be a royal blue alien.
The colour would remind you of the bright turquoise sky on a
summer's day.
If you went away from the alien
In the distance it would look like a blue jewel shining
And glistening attractively.

Ryan Michael Cook (9)
Brough Community Primary School, Kirkby Stephen

The Moon

What am I?
Night-brighter
Dream-maker
Star-lighter
Star-helper
Night-gazer
Star-seer
Bright-lighter
Star-provider
Night-bringer
Dream-giver
Spirit-raiser.

The moon.

Nathan Whittle (9)
Brough Community Primary School, Kirkby Stephen

Out Of This World

The galaxy is huge
With loads of stars.
Loads of planets
Including Mars

Shiny patterns full of light
Some people like to make a wish
When they see stars at night.

Slowly moving round and round
The Earth is moving
It is moving quietly without a sound.

Loads of planets in the sky
Waving the galaxy goodbye.

Samantha Bousfield (10)
Brough Community Primary School, Kirkby Stephen

Stars

Wish maker
Space sparkler
Light maker
Darkness lighter
Sky glistener
Night twinkler
Sky sparkler
Shooting sprinkler
Night flyer
Space soarer
Darkness leader.

Kane Tyler (10)
Brough Community Primary School, Kirkby Stephen

The Spaceman

He tied his lace
To go to outer space.
He flew through the stars
And played with the aliens on the Planet Mars.
But when he got to the moon
He landed with a *kaboom.*
Then he was sad
But he became glad
When he found his iPhone
And finally went back home.

Flynn Turnbull (11)
Brough Community Primary School, Kirkby Stephen

Black Hole

Light killer
Earth saver

Star killer
Sun guarder

Alien killer
Spaceship destroyer

Meteor killer
Black sucker.

Tom Turnbull (8)
Brough Community Primary School, Kirkby Stephen

The Moon

I am mind-blowing,
Other planets are bumpy.
Most people say I am rumbling,
But I think I am wavy.

I am quite chilly,
In the air the stars are colourful.
People stand on me and think the Milky Way is swirly,
That's OK, I know I am beautiful.

Samantha Jayne Margaret Bainbridge (10)
Brough Community Primary School, Kirkby Stephen

Out Of This World

Space unicorns soaring through the stars,
Delivering the rainbows all around the world,
Fighting crime, getting rid of alien slime,
In a short amount of time.
One over Uranus and one over Venus,
Leaving Mars behind bars!

Connor Evans (10)
Brough Community Primary School, Kirkby Stephen

What Am I?

Burning-redder,
Day-stayer,
Night-sleeper,
Skin-scalder,
Body-burner
Can't stretch any further,
Doesn't get any closer,
Holiday-thriller.

Isobel Dargue (11)
Brough Community Primary School, Kirkby Stephen

The Moon

What am I?
Night-bringer
Dark-maker
Star-helper
Night-master
Lonely-worker
Astonishing-lighter
The moon.

Alfie Rothery (11)
Brough Community Primary School, Kirkby Stephen

Moon

Bright light
Like diamonds in the sky,
Stars circle in the sky bright,
Whispering like mermaids
In the bright sun
Like a fire,
A glowing hot fire
In the sky.

Emily Davidson (8)
Brough Community Primary School, Kirkby Stephen

Sun And Moon

Sun
Large, bold
Boiling, scalding, shining
Giant star, sphere of cheese
Dazzling, shimmering, sparkling
Crystal sphere
Moon.

Olivia Moffat (9)
Brough Community Primary School, Kirkby Stephen

Star And Moon

Star
Bright, hot
Twinkling, shimmering, shining
Beacon in the sky, white sphere up high
Glowing, swaying, glittering
Quiet, calm
Moon.

Sophie Clapham (8)
Brough Community Primary School, Kirkby Stephen

Out Of This World

Immense planets flying through the air
Historical stars vast but rare
Crumbling craters floating into the atmosphere
As dark as a shut-down computer
Gloomy with a pinch of fear
Breathtaking world fluorescent and magic
Take off your mask and it could get tragic.

Barney Oliver Parsons (11)
Brough Community Primary School, Kirkby Stephen

Caitlin

C is for careful
A is for apples, my favourite
I is for interesting
T is for typing on the computer
L is for language
I is for instructions
N is for nice.

Caitlin Pedley (5)
Brough Community Primary School, Kirkby Stephen

Thomas

T is for tractor expert
H is for happy boy
O is for Oliver
M is for Max
A is for any
S is for shakes, my favourite is banana.

Thomas Steadman (6)
Brough Community Primary School, Kirkby Stephen

Jesika

J is for jelly wobbling
E is for elephant
S is for snake
I is for in my house
K is for Kit-Kat
A is for ant.

Jesika Pattinson (5)
Brough Community Primary School, Kirkby Stephen

Liam

L is for listening ears
I is for interesting
A is for awesome
M is for monkeys

I am a cheeky monkey.

Liam Pattinson (6)
Brough Community Primary School, Kirkby Stephen

Space

S ilver saucer in the sky – the things inside are really shy
P eople in rockets having a blast – as others fly slowly past
A lien Andy as sweet as a pansy
C andy Land is on the planet with the band
E ddie the Eagle could never fly so high!

Tom Davey (8)
Brough Community Primary School, Kirkby Stephen

Planets

S tars glimmer in the night sky
P lanets gloom in the darkness
A stronauts land on the moon
C lever aliens on Mars
E T parties on the moon every night.

Jack Dargue (8)
Brough Community Primary School, Kirkby Stephen

Space

S tars shine bright in the darkness
P lanet Earth is very warm
A liens pop up out of the moon
C ircles surround the moon
E arth is very high up.

Josie Beth Closs (7)
Brough Community Primary School, Kirkby Stephen

Maisy

M is for marvellous
A is for amazing
I is for inside playing
S is for swimming
Y is for young.

Maisy Brass (5)
Brough Community Primary School, Kirkby Stephen

Space

S tars shine brightly in the night sky
P lanets all around me in the gloomy dark
A liens popping up out of the moon
C ircles going around some of the planets
E meralds are in the holes of the moon.

Emma Pedley (7)
Brough Community Primary School, Kirkby Stephen

Space

S pace there is no gravity
P lanets are massive
A liens are scary
C an gravity keep you on the ground?
E meralds are here.

William Smith (8)
Brough Community Primary School, Kirkby Stephen

Beth

B is for beautiful
E is for excellent
T is for treats
H is for hungry.

Beth Evans (6)
Brough Community Primary School, Kirkby Stephen

Star

S hooting through space
T urtles with ten eyes
A liens having parties every night
S ir Ryan showing off to the planets.

Harris Lucas (9)
Brough Community Primary School, Kirkby Stephen

Eden

E is for every friend
D is for dog
E is for electricity
N is for no.

Eden Jack McDonald (6)
Brough Community Primary School, Kirkby Stephen

Indy

I is for intelligent
N is for nice to my friends
D is for dictionaries
Y is for yellow yo-yos.

Indy Brittleton (5)
Brough Community Primary School, Kirkby Stephen

Ewan

E is for eating a lot
W is for water, I go swimming
A is for astronaut, I like them
N is for nice, I am helpful.

Ewan Morrison (5)
Brough Community Primary School, Kirkby Stephen

Out Of This World!

O uter space is quiet and peaceful,
U nder and over the Earth it is,
T ouch the sun, touch the moon and what fun it would be to touch
the stars.

O ther planets dwarfed and red,
F or they are cool just like your bed.

T he sun is hot, more than your oven,
'H ello,' says the moon when dawn is here,
I n the sky, the moon is so beautiful,
S o bright is the sun, amazing it is.

W onderful worlds, all of them are,
O n the moon was Armstrong in 1969,
R ockets are the things that get us there,
L ong journeys people take to get there,
D own you look, at Earth.

William Knapp (9)
Croft CE Primary School, Darlington

On My Own

3, 2, 1 blast-off in my rocket,
I felt alone so I reached in my pocket,
I brought out a wrecked photo of mine and looked at it,
As I looked I felt astonished for a bit.

Suddenly I look out of my window and see
Everything I imagined it would be.
I saw fizzing, sparkling stars glowing in my eyes,
Then as I moved on I said goodbye.

Finally I got down from space,
I felt calm and very safe,
As I untied my lace
I said thank you space.

Harriet Foster (10)
Croft CE Primary School, Darlington

How I Wish I Was On The Moon Again

5, 4, 3, 2, 1 blast-off!
Off I flew in the emerald green rocket,
Soaring through the air at 100 miles per hour,
Goodbye gravity,
Goodbye Earth.

The moon is growing closer,
Stars like diamonds,
Sun like gold gliding through the air,
So close to the moon, *bang,*
I have landed on the moon!

How I wish I was on the moon again,
Moon rock and craters,
Aliens round corners just like it used to be,
I wish I was on the moon again.

Francesca Smith (9)
Croft CE Primary School, Darlington

My Dad Said

Earth is a planet in space!
Pluto is classified as a meteor!
The sun is a big burning star!
And I like driving in space cars!
My mum said,
'Pluto is classified as a planet!
Earth is a meteor in space!
The sun is a load of glow worms
And I like to drive in space cars!
And I said,
'That is all wrong Mum and Dad!
Pluto is a meteor behind Neptune!
Earth is covered in water!
And I like to drive in normal cars!'

Aiden Fortune (10)
Croft CE Primary School, Darlington

Space Night!

Bang! Whoosh! Don't turn around,
I've said goodbye,
I am off the ground,
Things are going sky-high.

Jupiter and Mercury,
Saturn and the sun,
All the things that I can see
Way up in the galaxy.

Tho moon is shining oh so bright,
The stars are winking down at me,
It really is the perfect night,
'Goodbye!' I scream, it was a sight.

Emily Rose Coates (10)
Croft CE Primary School, Darlington

Moon Mission!

My foot set on the crumbly ground,
For the moon I had found.

Earth was there, way below,
Cities stood with a wonderful glow.

Saturn's great rings clamped tighter and tighter,
Now I am so high, I feel much lighter.

The sun is like a blazing lamp,
It certainly wasn't cold and damp.

At last it's time to leave the moon,
'Goodbye,' I said, 'see you soon!'

Charlotte Rutter (11)
Croft CE Primary School, Darlington

Planet Earth

P owerful planets
L ovely like a flower
A wesome astronomy
N ice NASA
E pic Earth
T remendous like a black hole

E xcellent Earth
A s amazing as the Milky Way
R otating
T owering over you like a giant
H uge like the Pacific Ocean.

Evie Schmidt (9)
Croft CE Primary School, Darlington

Out Of Space!

O n the way to taking off
U nder the blanket keeping warm
T aking off, '3, 2, 1 blast-off!'

O ut of space looking at all the beautiful planets and stars
F ar, far away from home

S tepping on the moon floating in the air
P utting on a show for the aliens
A mazing sights from Mars
C an see all the stars blinking at me
E nding the mission and back home.

Ellie Bancroft (11)
Croft CE Primary School, Darlington

Wacky Planets!

My granny said
Earth is a nurse,
Sun is a nun,
Moon is a loon,
Mars is a bar
And black holes are holey.

And Mercury's mad,
Jupiter's jumping,
Noptune's being naughty
And the Milky Way is milking!

Adam Fitzhugh (11)
Croft CE Primary School, Darlington

Super Space

Twinkly-bright
Silently-sizzling
Wondrous-silent
Puddle-breaker
Asteroid-smasher
Ace in space
Darkness-changer
Light-bringer
Earth-illuminate
The sun.

Elsa Butler (10)
Croft CE Primary School, Darlington

Martians On The Moon . . .

Martians on the Moon
Crater boarding, they have fun
Racing in the dust.

Martians on the Moon
Chasing through the huge hills
They run back and forth.

Martians on the Moon
Gazing up at the bright sun
They tan their green cheeks.

Emma Craig (10)
Croft CE Primary School, Darlington

Space Mission

Blast-off
Up, up, up,
Clouds dancing goodbye,
I am in the ginormous galaxy,
As I move by the stars wink at me,
Whoosh up in the shocking space,
Aliens are playing on the moon,
As I leave the planets wave goodbye.
Space was ace.

Erin Wilson (10)
Croft CE Primary School, Darlington

My Wish Came True

Crash, poof
In the spaceship I go
Away from my family
Oh no!
Boom, bang what's that?
I couldn't believe my eyes
I had landed on the moon
Oh my wishes have come true!

Ebere Duru (9)
Croft CE Primary School, Darlington

Universe

U nharmed and untouched
N ever stop dreaming
I nfinite possibilities
V ery quiet, it is seeming
E vening, day or night? Impossible to tell
R ight and no wrong, not a bit
S oon you will know, very soon
E very moment counts, so treasure it.

Thomas Millar (11)
Croft CE Primary School, Darlington

Going To The Moon!

I watch the stars but also watch the TV
As they find the lost spacecraft which landed on Mars,
I get in the rocket and then look at my locket,
I land on the moon and the time is noon,
The sun shines, the stars are in weird lines.
I stick in the flag and then get my bag,
I hurry home, otherwise my parents will moan.

Mia Bicknell (11)
Croft CE Primary School, Darlington

Journey To The Moon

P lanets are moving cautiously through space
L anding bravely on the moon
A fter that, putting helmets on
N earing a black hole
E arth floating way down below
T he gravel crumbling beneath my feet
S topping to take in the silence.

Macy Howe (10)
Croft CE Primary School, Darlington

The Moon Is Like Cheese

The moon is like cheese.
The planets are like meatballs.
Gravity is like gravy.
Stars are like cars.
Shooting stars are the full tank cars.
Rockets are the crickets.

Jacob Alexander Michael Kearney (10)
Croft CE Primary School, Darlington

The Ace Space

S pace is ace and is better than your face
P lanets are all about pace because they turn and spin around the
sun
A re there actually aliens on planets?
C olourful, no not anymore when you're in space
E very day you think, *one day could I go in space?*

Gavan Singh Birk (10)
Croft CE Primary School, Darlington

Space

S tars sparkling brightly
P lanets move around the sun
A mazing moons are as beautiful as a diamond
C olourful rockets in the sky
E arth is down below.

Talia Rayner-Smith (11)
Croft CE Primary School, Darlington

The Enormous Silent Space

S pace is silent and gigantic
P lanets are tinier than the sun
A xis holds the heavy Earth
C olours are bright in the dark night
E xcellent space and excellent moon.

Lewis Monaghan (10)
Croft CE Primary School, Darlington

Space

S pace is ace
P lanets as hard as rock
A steroids as bumpy as a brick
C omet as fast as Usain Bolt
E xtraordinary.

Olivia Mulcrone (10)
Croft CE Primary School, Darlington

The Great Ace Space

S pace is ace
P lanets near and far
A steroids whizz off in their shuttles
C ommunication is crackly beyond Earth
E verything is black in the deep, dark ace space.

George Farrow (11)
Croft CE Primary School, Darlington

Sparkly Space!

S parkly space as beautiful as sequins
P lease don't be late
A t last you've arrived
C an you see the glistening stars?
E xcellent Earth, can you see it?

Ella Hirst (11)
Croft CE Primary School, Darlington

Untitled

They come from Mars with slime,
They lurk in the shadows at night.
Creeping up on you in the night,
Jumping on you but what are they?
While you walk along you hear footsteps behind you
But nothing's there when you look.
When you're asleep you hear noises,
They've come from Mars to fight.
They are ready for us but are we ready for them?
With their big slimy hands and big slimy body
Hopefully we will win the fight.
But we laze and hopefully we'll be prepared
Next time for the men from Mars.

Dylan Murray (10)
Esh Winning Primary School, Durham

Out Of This World

The luxurious, shimmering stars float in the darkness of space,
Stars are normally brilliant white, red or blue, telling their age,
They are scattered all around space,
Stars refer to Earth as a brilliant light blue light,
Stars are massive but look mini in the night.

The moon is a night-light pinching the sun's light,
It seems to change shape as it travels through the months,
Moons orbit planets like Earth.
Moons have dark sides where the sun cannot reach,
The shimmering, silver moon takes twenty-eight days to orbit the
Earth.

The colossal floating fireball,
Gets orbited by planets that look like they'll fall
And warms up the summer days for Earth,
The sun makes summers warm,
Like an oversized street lamp it shines brightly.

Do you know that planets are all different shapes and sizes?
Jupiter, Neptune, Mars, Pluto and Earth are some of the eight
planets.
There's some dwarf planets in the solar system too!
Planets are different colours, green and blue.
Rings and gases, hot and cold, each one different.

The wonderful galaxy has black holes!
The Milky Way is one place that'll be studied for eternity.
It is a glow of satisfaction,
Beyond the eye can see,
It's a whole new world,
That's where the interest begins.

Earth sending pings out to space,
To see if aliens will travel.
We could study them along with humans,

They might control minds.
Not everyone believes in aliens,
Can we be the only living beings?
What do aliens look like?
Nobody really knows!

Toni Walton (10)
Esh Winning Primary School, Durham

Out Of This World

A dark side of the moon
Orbiting the Earth for eternity
Craters dotted everywhere
Dangling in the abyss
A beam of satisfaction

No ending to this exquisite pearl
Twinkling like a human's eye
Glistening like a diamond
Trillions of light years!
Stars scattered aimlessly

Green people roaming the universe
People listen for these creatures
Are aliens real?
What do you think?

Eight planets to remember (and a few dwarfs!)
An array of colour
Big bouncy ball
Is there life?

Milky Way rushing through the solar system
Stars dying out
Sucking black holes
Never-ending skies

A beacon of light
Burning ball of fire
A ball being torched alight.

Cameron Wynne-Godeau (10)
Esh Winning Primary School, Durham

Out Of This World

Stars glistening,
Change colour,
Glistening skies,
And a pale blue dot,
As Earth satellites spin a path through the dark skies.

All eight planets spin with joy,
Some freezing cold,
Some are red hot,
But all are never forgot,
Eight planets spinning around,
All are big and bright,
The sun in the dark skies.

Beady eyes,
Wide mouth,
Big nose,
Can you guess?
Yes!
It's the moon,
The moon orbits the Earth,
Waxing and waning as the months flow by!

Twinkling and glistening, sparkling bright,
Stars sparkling bright,
In the night,
Twinkling and winkling and extremely bright,
How old are they, how long will they last in the dark skies?

The green, slimy UFOs call out to be captured,
Mankind evil critters with twenty eyes and twenty antennae,
They may be cute as lions,
But would you hide from the twenty-eyed critters
Coming from the dark skies?

Hannah Rippon (10)
Esh Winning Primary School, Durham

Out Of This World

The stunning stars,
Glisten with beauty,
Floating in the mild air, giving us unbuyable light,
So, so far away looks like they aren't even a mile away.

The sun is a burning ball of gas in the sky,
Yellow enormous ball of flames,
It gleams yellow light,
Gives us light and peace,
Gives us tans, gives us happiness.

The moon gives us tranquillity,
It has a dark side,
It has a settled stride,
Takes 28 days to orbit the sun,
When it is half it looks like a bun.

Planets come in all different sizes,
Over-sized bouncy balls,
Live in the solar system,
Some have loops, some do not.

Are aliens real or are they not?
Are they green, are they?
Have they ever been seen?
Every day people try to get communication with the aliens,
Will we ever hear back from them?

There are lots of galaxies such as Milky Way.
Mars, Venus, Jupiter and many more,
They are out of this world!
They are beyond the eye can see,
There is to be a black hole.

Bobby Guy (10)
Esh Winning Primary School, Durham

Out Of This World!

The stars
At night, watch the stars glitter in the night sky.
Shining like a torch,
Shining beautifully,
Will they last in the night sky?
The stars go as morning arrives.

The sun
The sun is flaming like a ball of fire,
Replacing the stars in the sky.
You don't want to go near it,
You will die because of the flaming ball of fire.
Nine planets get their heat from this flaming ball of fire.

The planets
Nine planets, now there are eight,
Planets like balls floating in space, all alone.
Enormous gas giants, solid masses of rock, rings of mystery,
All make our solar system, are we all alone?

The moon
The moon has two faces
And many phases
It resembles a banana,
Or a bouncing, floating ball,
Sometimes, hiding behind clouds,
But it is always there in the night sky.

The galaxy
The galaxy, what is out there? Who knows.
Our solar system, Venus, Neptune, Mars, sun, Earth and more,
The galaxy is enormous, floating alone in space.

Kyle Gregory (9)
Esh Winning Primary School, Durham

Out Of This World Poem!

The stars are shimmering in the darkness of the sky,
Twinkling in the moonlight,
They are origins of the universe,
Stars refer to Earth as tiny little dots,
The tiny little dots are glittery.

Sun is like a fireball burning through the sky,
It is a ball of burning gas,
The sun is giant and bright,
It lights up the sky at night.

The moon shines in the darkness of the night,
It changes shapes,
Waxing and waning as the months pass by,
Sea of tranquillity,
It's the glow of satisfaction.

The planets are like oversized beach balls,
Was there life, was there not?
Is there life, is there not?
Freezing cold, boiling hot?

There is a Milky Way (it is not a chocolate),
Studied for eternity by mankind,
In the galaxy there are different shades of stars,
Black hole,
The horoscopes are created,
Never-ending skies.
Aliens are apparently slimy and green,
They have never been seen,
Do you believe or not?
Scientists try and get to them.

Leah Finley (10)
Esh Winning Primary School, Durham

Out Of This World!

Stars, glistening, glimmering in the night!
Sleeping on tight schedules
As bright as the sun
Older than we thought.

Sun, as bright as metallic gold!
The humongous sun glistens in the day
A huge ball of gas and fire!
Here for all eternity.

Moon, the moon waxing and waning!
Orbits the Earth 24 hours of the day
Sea of tranquillity
It's so two-faced!
The moon has a dark side
And a bright side.

Planets, oversized bouncy balls are boiling!
Solar systems are like a desert without a camel!
The Milky Way swirls like a lollipop!
Studying for all eternity!

Galaxy, the galaxy is as big as a camel's hump!
It gets older and older!
The galaxy is like a chocolate bar!
Mysterious creatures live there!

Aliens, every day we are listening for communication!
They are analogue aliens!
There are funky green creatures!
Opinion or fact, real or not
We don't know.

Alfie Hart (10)
Esh Winning Primary School, Durham

Out Of This World

Stars glimmer with excitement,
As they wander through the never-ending abyss.
Black holes gulp up spacecrafts,
They don't know what is on the other side,
No one knows!

Astrologists studying galaxies,
For thousands of years.
Black holes disappear really fast,
When people go through.

Our galaxy is known as Milky Way,
Planets like over-sized beach balls.
There were nine planets but now there are eight,
There are eight planets in all,
Earth is the only watered surface in our solar system.

The moon's craters act like facial features,
One side is dark; the other is laminated by the sun's light,
This gives it two faces.
What is your opinion about aliens?
Do you or don't you believe aliens are real?
Astrologists have been spending billions of pounds
To prove to the public that aliens are real.
The stars are glistening with brightness
As they wander around never-ending abyss,
They shine as bright as a golden pearl.

The sun is like a flaming ball of fire,
No one has ever been near the sun before
As it can seriously burn you.

Aaron Stead (10)
Esh Winning Primary School, Durham

Robotic War

One normal day . . .
Date: 21st December 2012,
Robotic creatures coming from space,
We can't do this, we're softer than clay.
Crash, boom!
They're against us,
What are we going to do?

Out comes the green goblin-like creatures,
We are unsure about their features.
Zap, zap, zap!
We have to fight!

When our world comes to war,
We will never give up,
We will protect our core.
This is truly a robotic war.

But when scientists discover
They will uncover,
A giant dragon-like robot,
With a green slimy creature inside,
And on its head there is a pot.
This is truly a robotic war.

Boom!
Was that us or was it them?
There's no world left
Or other people.
Where am I?
That was truly a robotic war.

Josh Harker (10)
Esh Winning Primary School, Durham

The Little Green Men From Mars

The ships soon came,
Closer and closer,
The creatures come out,
Nearer and nearer,
They try to come in peace,
But are drowned out by screams,
The little green men from Mars . . .

They come out with frowns,
Search through towns,
Trying to find new friends,
They search round bends,
Find some hens,
They soon run away,
The little green men from Mars . . .

After two days of looking,
They find their new friend,
It's a human named Mark.
More ships come,
The ships are screaming,
Like the humans,
The little green men from Mars . . .

The captain said he wanted his men,
So we handed them over,
Glooming lights flying away,
Galaxies away, they live another day,
Will we ever see them again?
The little green men from Mars . . .

Andrew Powell (10)
Esh Winning Primary School, Durham

They Came From Planet Elesa!

Nowhere to run?
Nowhere to hide?
Will they rip through until they find where you lie?
Are these the men from Mars?
Maybe, but we don't know yet,
All we know is, they've come to destroy Earth!

'Roll out the tanks,
Bring out the jets,
Wo nood to destroy this fleet,
Otherwise we'll be dead meat!'

Will we be able to defeat them?
Maybe,
They've got high-tech weaponry,
But we've got the will to live on,
And we're not gonna give up,
As long as we've got the light and the sun,
It's not going to happen . . .
Wait, is that the mothership?

What's it saying?
They're from Planet Elesa!
Oh, we're done for now,
Because they're the huge overlords!

Aidan Kirkup (11)
Esh Winning Primary School, Durham

Out Of This World

Did you know that planets come in all shapes and sizes,
Some are small and some are big.
They are like a desert with no camel
Or the North Pole with no penguins and no snow.

This is the sun, it glimmers and shimmers in the daydream sky,
And as the moon is lightly peeking through the clouds for thousands
of years
The sun has risen about eight o'clock every morning
It's like my shining star.

I glow in the night just like a night light
And glow with all my joy, I rise at four on a school night,
I'm like a gold trophy standing on the fire.

I'm like a banana floating in the air
And help you get to sleep in the night
And I like to light the sky up at night.

I'm the galaxy and I would like to meet you
So come and see my black hole and my Milky Way
So we could make you tea and coffee
And I can make you something to eat.

We are the aliens and we would like to come and see you soon
When you receive the beep and you will hopefully find us one day.

Melanie-Leigh Watson (10)
Esh Winning Primary School, Durham

Out Of This World

Stars are like sparkles in the night sky;
Stars twinkling in the moonlight,
Every night the stars change beautifully.

The moon is like a cold ball,
Orbiting the Earth,
Glowing with satisfaction.

The sun is like a fireball burning in the sky,
Sun giving light to our exquisite world.

Planets are like bouncy balls in the sky,
There are big ones,
Medium ones and small ones,
All different sizes and colours.

Aliens are green and very slimy,
Opinions or fact, are they real or not?
What colour are they, green, black, red or blue?

The galaxy has the Milky Way,
Studied for eternity,
Whilst floating in never-ending skies.

Poppy Taylor
Esh Winning Primary School, Durham

Space

Take a trip to space and see planets,
And stars fly past the window of your rocket.
Gas giants orange and blue Jupiter,
Saturn, Neptune and Mercury.

Humans wrinkle, stars just twinkle,
Stars change colour when they get older,
And the red star is the oldest star
You can get before it explodes.

Galaxies are groups of stars
That take you to a new dimension,
Which is awesome.

Aliens are hopefully real
And I want to meet one,
Even if it is evil,
They must be real but in a different galaxy.

The moon is very small in the galaxy
And there is more than one moon.
The moon is really small compared to Earth.

Liam Bersey
Esh Winning Primary School, Durham

The Day When The Creatures Arrived

One day something bad happened,
Nothing but a tense darkness,
It was Independence Day,
That was the day when the creatures arrived.

Crashing from the sky,
They thought it was a star,
It was a creature,
It spread an infection, causing one million people to die,
That was the day when the creatures arrived.

Then more started to come,
The great battle has begun,
That was the day when the creatures arrived.

After the war they thought they had won,
Time after time we tracked them down,
We had to hide, no food, no water,
Just death,
That is when we died.

Robson Kershaw (11)
Esh Winning Primary School, Durham

Out Of This World Attack

They were furry, with the horns of a deer,
It had the stripes of a tiger,
Beak of a bird, I was full of fear,
With the legs of a panda, we could not cheer.

It ate bugs,
But not slugs.

Not very active, it would often sleep,
Shoot when it rested, ammo we needed to keep,
Piercing horns we could not beat,
Nowhere to hide, we were dead meat,
Nothing left to fight for, we had to accept defeat.

Ben Patterson (11)
Esh Winning Primary School, Durham

Out Of This World

When we see stars what do we think?
I think of different colours and glittering lights.
Floating in the sky, oh so bright.
How pretty, how pretty, lovely to see, lovely to see for me.

When we see the moon what do we think?
I think of a floating night light giving away precious light.
Orbiting the Earth for eternity,
How pretty, how pretty, lovely to see, lovely to see for me.

When we see planets what do we think?
I think of oversized bouncy balls with or without rings.
Is there life on these planets, who knows?
How pretty, how pretty, lovely to see, lovely to see for me.

When we see the sun what do we think?
I think of sizzling fire on the enormous planet,
Burning anything that comes near.
How pretty, how pretty, lovely to see, lovely to see for me.

Sophie Simpson (10)
Esh Winning Primary School, Durham

Men From The Galaxy

In 2030, the world is a peaceful place,
Crash-landing in a small Scottish village,
Was it a huge meteor?

Soon after landing it opened,
It was an army of men from the galaxy.
Everyone thought they were cute
But when they were asleep the men from the galaxy turned evil.

The bells rang which means they are evil men from the galaxy.
Everybody ran and got into rockets
But the bravest men stayed behind
To win the village back.

Ellie Gillies (11)
Esh Winning Primary School, Durham

The Attack From Space

Long legs,
Fighting feet,
Attacking an innocent planet,
Destroying 2025 on Earth.

Out comes giant squirrels,
Huge teeth,
Immensely sized claws,
Just for ripping human beings to shreds!
Destroying 2025 on Earth.

People with only weapons,
To kill the amazing things,
Destroying 2025 on Earth.

The things are full of colour,
Coming in fleets,
They are creatures from the universe,
Destroying 2025 on Earth.

Shay Liddell-Kenny (11)
Esh Winning Primary School, Durham

The Things Are Coming

It's 2003, everyone is running,
More things are coming and they said it would never happen.
Meteor spaceships crash into the ground.
The things are coming, you better run and hide.

Red eyes, four legs, what more do they want?
Dangerous, evil, metal things,
Taking over the world!
Galaxy, black hole, don't know where they come from?

One man, a brave man stayed behind,
Fighting, killing, who knows what will happen?
The things are coming, you better run for your life!

Hannah McGovern (10)
Esh Winning Primary School, Durham

2080

A normal day in 2080
People seeing spaceships lately.
This thing landed,
Now stranded,
But wait!
Something's coming . . .

Look at that greenish skin
The foreign language and its carrying a . . . bin?
Suddenly, screaming, shouting from all around,
Not the most pleasant welcome,
Must be because they've just been found
But wait . . .
They have no weapons,
Instead . . . flowers
They want peace!

Lauren Emmerson (11)
Esh Winning Primary School, Durham

The Green, Gooey, Gloomy Attack

Crash, crash, crash, crash,
They have landed,
They're here, run!
It's the men from Mars.

He said they will never come,
But they're here,
Do they want peace or war,
It's the men from Mars.

They want war,
They're going to kill us all,
They are like lions coming to kill,
They want out heat,
It's the men from Mars,
Help!

Jasmine Gregory (10)
Esh Winning Primary School, Durham

Men Of Mars

Men of Mars have landed,
Men of Mars have come,
One million died,
Men of Mars, there's none.

Men of Mars want a battle,
We're ready for a hassle,
But the men of Mars won,
Men of Mars won,
Mon of Mars won,
Now it's time for fun!

Men of Mars retreated,
Back to where they came,
They never will attack again,
Because we have won,
We have won,
We have won.

Men of Mars never came again,
We had won.

Bradlee Peart (11)
Esh Winning Primary School, Durham

The Green, Gooey Attack

There was a green gooey thing
Floating in the air,
A green man who floats,
Green and gooey came from Mars,
Who knows, they might have come from the stars.

We come in peace,
We do not harm,
The green people who float,
And wear big black coats,
They fly away and live another day,
Then suddenly they fade away.

Niamh Lamb (10)
Esh Winning Primary School, Durham

Stars

Oh stars, tiny, big, small.
Oh to be far, you look like a ball.
Oh in the black night sky I see you there.
I know you're bigger than a bear.

Oh how I know you live in space
And I live on Earth.
Oh time has passed
As rockets blast.

Oh star I see you are yellow.
Oh and you shine tonight
With your one delight.
I know a little twinkle when I see it.

Star so bright.
How I see you now.
I peer through a glance
As I see your little dance.

Abbie Elizabeth Reveley (8)
Kirkbampton CE Primary School, Carlisle

The Planets

Sun as wide as the smooth, heavy moon
Sun as boiling and bright as roaring, scorching fire
Sun as light and beautiful as sky so blue
Sun staring at round colourful Earth.

I am going to the breathtaking, shining moon
I know that I will be there soon
Wow, what's that noise? I can hear a happy, bright tune
What's that wonderful smell? It smells of perfume.

After the round moon I am going to the colourful Earth
Right now I actually feel like I want to go to Jupitor
What's that beautiful loud noise saying 'hi'?
It sounds like a rocket zooming by.

Look at those bright silky stars
Right now I am staring at breathtaking Mars
It would be a lot safer now if I was in a sparkling car
Please stars, tell me that I'm nearly at Mars.

My mum and dad are going to be extra proud of me
The sea is deeper than the Earth though
I want to go on my space rocket now and go home
Now I will say bye to the planets and twinkling stars.

Shannon Leah Rowley (9)
Kirkbampton CE Primary School, Carlisle

Out Of This World

Darkness spreads as I step out of the rocket,
I could see the dust sweep at my feet.
I felt so high and the feel of the rock is in my grasp,
As I walk I can see where the planets meet.

The sun is like a blazing fireball blinding,
The stars sparkling in the void of darkness.
The moon so beautiful, silver and grey,
All the stars, planets, moon, sun and the solar system is anonymous.

Rosie Irving (10)
Kirkbampton CE Primary School, Carlisle

The Sun

Burning sun scorching round the sky,
Red hot glowing through the ice cold sky,
Red hot fire throwing down the sky,
Shaking the Earth like a meteor hitting the sky.

The burning, glowing ground,
Making the sun shake the ground,
The sun came down,
Like an avalanche hit the ground.

Burning hot sun,
Bright like a star,
The sun is a fireball,
The sun is a star.

Joe French (9)
Kirkbampton CE Primary School, Carlisle

In Space

Burning sun scorching round the sky,
Rockets whizzing by the rising sun,
The planets versus the sun,
Heat bursting past the planets.

Stars twinkling at their best,
Rockets landing on the moon,
Astronauts looking at the beautiful view,
People building rockets.

Stars sparkle past the planets,
Astronauts fixing the rockets,
Food floats around,
Burning, boiling sun.

Harriet Swailes (9)
Kirkbampton CE Primary School, Carlisle

The Perfect Planets

Plain grey Mercury sits silently,
Marvellous Mercury moves slowly,
Blazing light blue Neptune like a dot in the black sky,
Neptune sits so lonely.

Earth makes the solar system pop with excitement,
Earth, the most colourful planet of them all,
Jupiter, stripy as a zebra,
Jupiter, my favourite planet I call.

Pluto is a dwarf planet,
Nobody knows about Pluto, it's a mystery,
Red is the colour of Mars,
Mars, the big ball of fire, that's its history.

Rachel Long (10)
Kirkbampton CE Primary School, Carlisle

The Popping Planets

Beautiful, boiling sun
Shiny spaceships race about
Speeding over the gloomy moon, having fun
Tiny, twinkling stars shooting up.

Whirling round Saturn's icy ring
Golden shiny strands
Loudly and happily we sing
Bouncing around, off we go.

Jupiter, big and bright
Stripes of white and deep red
Leaping up and down lightly
Racing through the sapphire sky, off we go.

Rebecca Holliday (10)
Kirkbampton CE Primary School, Carlisle

Awesome Astronauts

Up in the night sky awesome astronauts flying by
In the midnight sky all you can see is a mist of light
The mist of light disappears into nothing
Awesome astronauts in roaring rockets alone and scared.

Awesome astronauts getting their suits on ready to go
Ready for the landing on the moon all is calm
Everything is ready but all is going terribly slow
If you look up in the sky you will see something flying.

Super soft scented suits smells all lovely
Rockets rumbling, roaring, ready to fly off
Flying through the universe, step by step
Rumbling, rocking on the moon.

Alice Tyson (10)
Kirkbampton CE Primary School, Carlisle

Unknown Universe

Burning, boiling, bright big sun,
Land on the moon to get the job done,
Shiny, shooting stars in the endless universe,
No gravity on the moon, just bounce.

The Earth is sapphire, emerald and white,
When you float in space you feel light,
The solar system can be interesting,
The moon's craters are fascinating.

The twinkling, bright stars,
The planet that is reddish brown is Mars,
Many rockets zooming in space,
Many planets, many stars.

Gabrielle Henshaw (9)
Kirkbampton CE Primary School, Carlisle

Zooming Rocket

I glance up to the sky so high
I really, really wish I could fly
I really, really like today
Because I can have my wonderful way.

I was zooming up so high
And it felt like I could fly
I didn't know which button I pressed
So I just decided to do my best.

I was looking in the oil tank
And it looked very, very blank
I was up very, very high
Very, very high up in the sky.

Evie Holden (8)
Kirkbampton CE Primary School, Carlisle

Away From Home

Space is dark, it's like a shark,
It eats you in a second.

Sun is hot, it's like a pot,
Bubbling on a stove.

The stars are bright diamonds in the sky,
They're away from home so very, very high.

Neptune is as blue as the sea,
All the planets in our galaxy.

Emma Walby (8)
Kirkbampton CE Primary School, Carlisle

Amazing Rockets

Roaring rockets fly through the sky,
Amazing rockets race up so high,
Burning rockets shoot flames so low,
Many rockets zoom up so fast.

I really wish I could fly,
To the Moon circling by,
Land on its bright, shiny rock,
As it moves around the Earth.

Mia Donald (9)
Kirkbampton CE Primary School, Carlisle

The Planet

Hot like flames
Boiling red sun
Flames like fire
Sun bursting with shine

Humongous bold planet
Jupiter, as big as a boulder
Stripy, dull colours
As strong as rock.

Emily Russell (8)
Kirkbampton CE Primary School, Carlisle

Twinkling Stars

Burning hot sun up in space.
Rockets zooming past
No gravity in place
Astronauts bouncing on the moon
As the moon orbits the Earth
Twinkling stars like floating diamonds
Planets moving in space.

William Long (8)
Kirkbampton CE Primary School, Carlisle

Planets

Big rocket flying so high
The red hot sun rising up into the sky
The people saying bye
The blue sky shining in space.

Mars up high in the sky
Stars sparkling in space
Satellites rolling around Earth
The moon controlling Earth.

Drew Allan (10)
Kirkbampton CE Primary School, Carlisle

The Rockets

Red rocket flying so high
Like a blaze into the sapphire sky
NASA sorting the satellite
In a hurry to the moon before the Soviet's blue rocket.

Blue rocket, the Soviet's journey to the moon as well
Just about to eject in space
Now they're neck and neck
On the famous race to space.

George Andrew Sproat (9)
Kirkbampton CE Primary School, Carlisle

The Sun

As hot as electricity
As hot as fire
It is fascinating
And boiling, steaming hot.

It is the hottest star
Gleaming, glooming
It lights the Earth
Wondrous and lovely.

Dylan Norman (8)
Kirkbampton CE Primary School, Carlisle

Rocky Mars

Rocket, rocket, fly to Mars
Listen to that rocket zoom
Nearly there, seeing stars
We arrive at our rocky planet.

We have arrived at our destination
Rocky, sandy Mars' texture
Looking up at the constellation
Rocket, rocket, you go home.

Josh Stirling (10)
Kirkbampton CE Primary School, Carlisle

Outer Space

Far space, freezing us as it glows
Blue rocket blows as it goes
In the dark blue sky stars shine
Racing, zooming through the sky.

Faster and faster, searching the galaxies
The universe as big as anything
Endless worlds out there, all alone
Spacemen far away, trying to get home.

Thomas Sawdon (9)
Kirkbampton CE Primary School, Carlisle

Space And Beyond

S pace is infinite
P lanets and stars everywhere
A steroids left, right and centre
C omets that aim for planets
E verything in motion

A stronomical society stares to the skies
N eptune, Saturn, there's a lot more
D arkness surrounds the solar system

B eyond Earth is a whole new world
E verlasting darkness through the galaxy
Y ellow sun burns my eyes
O ne dwarf planet, that's Pluto
N ever seen galaxies that haven't been discovered
D ark, never-ending. That is what space is.

Tyler Cornish (10)
Lowca Community School, Whitehaven

Space

A river of stars in the darkness
Planets being born
Our galaxy is exploding
The sun burning
The stars are twinkling
Black holes sucking
No life forms detected
Planets orbiting
Aliens hiding
People finding
Rockets flying
Asteroids crashing
The moon shining
Every minute timing.

Dylan Rhys Hodgson (8)
Lowca Community School, Whitehaven

Aliens

Star ships rocketing through space,
I hope the aliens don't have hate,
What if I get a mate?
Aliens having a race,
Planets, beautiful in the dark,
My rocket just got hit by a spark,
Neptune, Pluto and more,
I think I see an alien paw.

Leoni Hardwick (11)
Lowca Community School, Whitehaven

Earth

E veryone lives here,
A ll plants grow,
R ivers of water flowing down,
T winkling stars you can see,
H owever we travel out in rockets?

Dominic Ormerod (7)
Lowca Community School, Whitehaven

Oh Saturn

Oh Saturn, a gigantic icy ring.
Oh Saturn, what a brilliant thing.
Oh Saturn, how bright do you shine?
Oh Saturn, please will you be mine?

Oh Saturn, no other planet compares,
Oh Saturn, none of them ever dares.
Oh Saturn, are you the boss of them all?
Oh Saturn, why do none of you fall?

Oh Saturn, what an enchanted place,
Oh Saturn, that a mighty round face,
Oh Saturn, a huge swirly sphere,
Oh Saturn, you have no fear.

Oh Saturn, we have never visited your land,
Oh Saturn, can we give you a hand'?
Oh Saturn, you are a mystery,
Oh Saturn, why won't you tell me?

Charlotte Davison (10)
Mowbray Primary School, Choppington

Christmas Story – Haikus

Christmas is coming
It is beginning to snow
But Father's still gone

The day that he left
The leaves were yellow and red
Autumn has arrived

The present he left
We could not ever forget
T'was the gift of love

We sat in the house
Watching the cat and the mouse
Three more days to go

The girl was called Rose
Her brother was named Johnny
They need each other

Their mother was ill
And their dad may not return
He went off to war

Putting up the tree
Hanging tinsel on the door
Brings no joy to us

Two more days to go
Stockings are on the fireplace
Dad is still not back

One more day to go
It's gonna be amazing
But not without Dad

The day is now here
Guess who came through the front door?
Dad is back from war!

Molly Kennedy (10)
Mowbray Primary School, Choppington

One In A Million

There's a star in the sky
That rules the world,
As white as milky cream.

Though as there's millions
In the sky,
It's nowhere to be seen!

As I pass through the night
I wonder who will come next,
All of a sudden, as if by magic
A rocket comes, quite complex.

Weird people step off the rocket,
Carrying all of their things,
There was an alien and a robot
But suddenly there was a loud zing!

The robot picked up her phone
And said, 'Yes Mum, we're here!
I remembered the lemonade
And Dad remembered his beer.'

As they set up their tent
The atmosphere greeted them
By making a flower out of stars
With an extremely long stem.

After a while the weird people left
It was hard to say goodbye,
They jumped back into their rocket
And flew into the sky.

Oh I wonder what will happen next,
Galaxy galore,
Every day we love you space,
More and more and more!

Natalie Thompson (10)
Mowbray Primary School, Choppington

Dog Diary

Hey there, you'll never guess what,
This morning the fire was very hot,
Then I started to shiver and jeer,
So I said, 'Let's get out of here!'

But it was too late,
As I started to shake.

I shot up the chimney,
Said bye to Jimney.
I went so high,
I thought I would die!

I burst though the extremely strong atmosphere,
Forgetting about heights, my number one fear.
Earth seemed so far,
Then I heard a big roar!

It was a big green Martian,
His name was Old Cartian.
We started talking,
As we were walking.

I suddenly realised something was on my tail,
When I saw what it was I started to wail.
My tail was on fire!
It must've happened when I went higher.

It looked so amazing,
I started star-gazing,
I looked around me,
I felt tremendously happy.

The stars are still shining,
But I'm going to have to end this poem,
Because I've run out of words
That follow the rhyming.

Roan Hays (10)
Mowbray Primary School, Choppington

Extraterrestrials

Extraterrestrials, what a finding,
If I knew one, that would be exciting.

You may be small, compared to me,
I'm tall,
But if you want a friend, I'm who to call.

It's sci-fi, sci-fi,
All the scientists cry,
It's sci-fi, sci-fi,
I wish I could fly
In the UFOs you ride.

Space, oh space, the alien place
Now I can fly,
In this rocket high.

So, up I go,
With bricks on my toes,
There is no gravity,
To me it seems like insanity.

Aliens, now that I've met you,
I know what to do,
Don't talk in English,
You won't have a clue.

And now that I've landed,
I feel abandoned,
I don't know what is worse,
Than not seeing you on Earth.

Jasmine Claudia MacKellar (10)
Mowbray Primary School, Choppington

There Is A Place

There is a place where the aliens run,
There is a place where you always have fun,
No teachers, no rules,
No pests, only fools!

'Work your hardest,
Do your best.'
If this is what you want
Then what's the rest?

There is a place where the aliens run,
There is a place where you always have fun,
No teachers, no rules,
No pests, only fools!

Space, space, it's a magical place,
You should come and visit us all,
The Big Dipper, Orion's Belt,
I wonder if there's any more?

There is a place where the aliens run,
There is a place where you always have fun,
No teachers, no rules,
No pests, only fools!

Stars are bright,
They bring light,
I'm sure I'd be lost without them,
If they weren't there, what would we do?
I'm sure I'd be lost without them.

Caitlyn Hankinson (10)
Mowbray Primary School, Choppington

My Adventure

Here we go into space!
What a dark fantastic enchanted place.
The rocket floating in mid-air,
And I'm just sitting in my chair.

At last we've landed, here we are,
Oh look there's Earth, it's very far.
How on Earth will I get back?
Shall I use my amazing jetpack?

I'll scoop some cheese from the moon,
I'll be back home very soon.
Time to get inside my rocket,
I've got some cheese tucked in my pocket.

As I'm floating in the air,
My body's wobbling everywhere.
I'm almost through the atmosphere,
So I'll give off a great loud cheer!

Kate Appleby (10)
Mowbray Primary School, Choppington

The Destroyer – A Tsunami

Light-absorber
Fun-destroyer
Death-maker
Window-breaker
Country-waker
Nation-waterer
Piglet-slaughterer
People-walker
Rain-layer
World-sweeper

A tsunami.

Jay Taylor (10)
Mowbray Primary School, Choppington

Enchanting Love

My heart aches to see your smile,
You have been gone for quite a while.
Your love is so enchanting,
Unlike mine.

You are travelling over sea,
I just wish you would not be,
You are as sweet as sugar,
Unlike me.

You're still stuck in my mind,
I think that you might find
My love is unforgivable,
But you are just so kind.

You will very soon be back,
You are starting to pack,
Your love is so enchanting
And apparently so is mine.

Molly Kennedy (10) & Rosie
Mowbray Primary School, Choppington

What Am I?

Life-taker
House-burner
Light-bringer
Alarm-setter
Smoke-creator
Ash-maker
Risk-taker
Warmth-bringer
Food-provider
Perma frost-melter

A fire.

Aleysha Jade Harness (11)
Mowbray Primary School, Choppington

Me, Myself And I

Like a rose bush full of thorns,
I'll scratch and sharpen,
Like a silver kitchen knife,
I'll cut and sharpen,
Like me, myself and I,
I'll sharpen.

I'll be a landmine,
I'll explode,
Like a grenade,
I'll explode,
Like me, myself and I,
I'll explode.

I'll take it in the heart,
But in the moment,
It'll happen,
And I won't fall . . .

Rebecca Rose Swan (11)
Mowbray Primary School, Choppington

Who Am I?

Goal-keeper
Newcastle-player
Sunderland-hater
St James' Park-lover
Selfie-taker
Ball-saver
Holland-originator
Time-spender
Hair-fusser
Bean-pole.

A: Tim Krul.

Erin White (10)
Mowbray Primary School, Choppington

Horse Kennings

What am I?

Family-lover
Grass-eater
Fast-jogger
Chin-layer
Hand-licker
Carrot-eater
Pen-stayer
Human-follower
Field-lover
Cold-hater
Warm-lover
Heavy-sleeper

A horse.

Deanna Allison (11)
Mowbray Primary School, Choppington

Oh I Wonder, I Wonder

Stars shining bright in the sky,
Probably going to see them tonight,
Glistening, sparkling, twinkling light,
I wonder, I wonder,
If I'll see them tonight,
They could be dancing and prancing,
On their sparkly feet,
Oh I wonder, I wonder what they eat?
They might eat cheese or popcorn,
They might eat peas or feet!
Oh I wonder, I wonder what they eat?
They could be fat, they could be chubby,
They could be slim, they could be funny,
Oh I wonder, I wonder what they are?

Jack Lee (9)
Mowbray Primary School, Choppington

Planet Earth

P lanets, planets are everywhere in space.
L ife is everywhere in some dark, magical worlds.
A stronauts discover mind-blowing planets up in space.
N eptune is one of the medium-sized planets.
E arth is one of the smallest planets but where would we be without Earth?
T he sun is colourful to light the sky in space to show what it's worth.

E arn a rocket to see what space is really like.
A rocket can fly higher than birds and kites.
R ound the world goes and around we go.
T he world spins day and night but when does it ever sleep?
H undreds of people want to go to space, I would want to be the lucky one.

Laura Bisset (10)
Mowbray Primary School, Choppington

What Am I?

Water-destroyer
Wave-destructor
Animal-killer
Unnoticeable-threatener
City-wrecker
Water-master
Life-ender
Sea-swallower
Me-engulfer
People-terrifier

A tsunami.

Jemma Joslin (10)
Mowbray Primary School, Choppington

Me!

Loud-talker
Lush-singer
Green Day-listener
Nirvana-lover
Pizza-eater
Hair-player
Bad-listener
Friend-lover
One-Directioner
Fan-girler
That is the crazy me!

Zara Sophie Todd (11)
Mowbray Primary School, Choppington

What Am I?

Puddle-maker
Sadness-donator
Cold-creator
Beach-destroyer
Sky-darkener
Window-washer
Umbrella-needer
Rainbow-starter
Garden-feeder

The rain.

Emma Burns (10)
Mowbray Primary School, Choppington

What Am I?

Death-causer
Earth-quaker
Destruction-maker
Car-breaker
House-destroyer
Animal-killer
Human-drowner
Holiday-ruiner
Happiness-taker

A tsunami.

Ellie Davidson (10)
Mowbray Primary School, Choppington

What Am I?

Pie-eater
Bad-singer
Player-cheerer
Food-waver
Team-believer
Song-starter
Stairway-climber
Game-watcher
Manager-hater

A football supporter.

Daniel Wilkins (11)
Mowbray Primary School, Choppington

Planet Rock

P lanets are loud, planets are huge.
L isten, listen, listen carefully.
A band is playing all night long.
N ight is here.
E ntering the zone of rock.
T he aliens play all night long, you can almost hear them sing.

R ock must be their thing.
O h, what a sight it was, to see them dancing.
C ome and see them and their groovy moves.
K ind and caring, tiny aliens dancing on the moon.

Caitlin Rose Hall (10)
Mowbray Primary School, Choppington

A Monkey Called Harry

A monkey called Harry
Had a dog friend called Larry.
They went to the park
And ate some tree bark.
They dived into the river
And then started to shiver.
They met a cat who had a hat
And was walking with a rat!
The rat was quite fat
And he was lying on a chair!

Jayden Millican (10)
Mowbray Primary School, Choppington

Newcastle

N ew fantasy football team
E ven better than Barcelona
W ith players better than Messi and Ronaldo
C ost over £500,000,000
A ll games won
S taying at St James'
T ill the end
L ove the Geordies
E verlasting.

Warren Stuart (10)
Mowbray Primary School, Choppington

Dinosaurs

D is for dinosaur large and strong
I is for ignosaurus
N is for nigersaurus and nodosaurus
O is for our world, used to be the land of the dinosaurs
S is for stegosaurus, the mighty dinosaur
A is for a life which for a dinosaur is hard
U is for us and them, the dinosaurs
R is for residents of an asteroid hitting the planet
S is for say goodbye . . .

Ben Martin (11)
Mowbray Primary School, Choppington

The Owl

The sun dies, it is dark
I rise from my hole in the bark

I never leave my group of five
As I look to the deep black sky

I run, I jump, I swoop, I fly
As I glide through the night

The angel of dark has taken flight.

Cameron Bisset (11)
Mowbray Primary School, Choppington

A Gorilla Called Jeff

A gorilla called Jeff was close to his death,
So he explored the world,
He went to the sun,
Then went to the moon,
Then to a jungle and met a baboon,
The jungle was boring,
The baboon was snoring,
So the gorilla called Jeff left in the morning . . .

Finlay Batey (10)
Mowbray Primary School, Choppington

Dougie

Cat-chaser
Barks-never
Sleeping-snorer
Runner-racer
Beach-lover
Toy-player
Little-wonder!

Amye Louise Richardson (11)
Mowbray Primary School, Choppington

Duck

He is big and fat,
As a matter of fact.
He loves eating bread,
It has a tiny head.
He lives in the water,
He's a bit of a daughter.
He scares all the seagulls,
He acts like an eagle.

Callum Wolf (10)
Mowbray Primary School, Choppington

My Best Mate

I found my best mate
On my plate,
He was mashed in with my steak
Which I baked,
I ate him by mistake
But it turned out he was fake
And I was sick in the lake!

Flynn Thompson (11)
Mowbray Primary School, Choppington

Shark – Haiku

Skin as tough as a whale
Would not want to be near him
Bloodthirsty killer

Toughest in the sea
Stronger than a killer whale
Very dangerous.

James Pringle (11)
Mowbray Primary School, Choppington

Burger Acrostic

B rown burnt beef
U nhealthy but delicious
R otten from restaurants
G reasy grills
E veryone loves them
R elish on top.

Jack Annison (11)
Mowbray Primary School, Choppington

Zombie Acrostic

Z any swinger
O n a night, high flying
M onster of the night
B rain tucked up tight
I n a cave I lay
E nd up burning in the day, in the sun.

Adam Michael Hogg (11)
Mowbray Primary School, Choppington

My Guide

Guardian angel
Pure and bright
Guard me while I sleep tonight
Even when you're awake I'm here
And when I'm here it's all clear.

Abigail Turner (11)
Mowbray Primary School, Choppington

The Wolf – Haiku

Sharp teeth, lots of fur,
Blue eyes watching from afar,
Running like the wind!

Michael Davis (10)
Mowbray Primary School, Choppington

My Crazy Out Of This World Imagination

The space awaits me to fill it in, I will . . .
Use some glitter to create the stars,
Part of some navy blue carpet,
To create the space.
And to craft the planets I will . . .
For Saturn craft a blue-grey clay ball then,
Put an onion ring around it.
And for Mars I'll use a sweet potato and roll it in sand.
To craft constellations I'll use some fire-red string
And dip it in ripped up foil.
Then to make the sun I will use an orange hamster's exercise ball,
And put sharp spikes all over it.
To make the moon I'll use a bumpy golf ball.
And finally, to make the most beautiful of all . . .
A star cluster I'll mix some multicoloured cake sprinkles,
Silver sequins that glisten,
Sand and dust,
And last but not least,
Some hair spray to represent mighty gas clouds!

But all in all, this is just my crazy out of this world imagination!

Niamh Challoner (11)
Our Lady Star Of The Sea RCVA Primary School, Peterlee

Planet Galax

Fog covers the moist ground.
Lasers heading towards the palace of Galax.
Guards trying to fight back but struggle.
Martians running for their lives.
Bombs in the background.
Martians stop and look.
Their city is gone.
The princess runs towards them.
The only royal survivor.
The ship glides towards them.
Everyone hides quickly.
A storm is coming; they dig a hole to hide in.
Waves crashing across the mossy rocks.
Trees falling down;
Hitting the ships, destroying them.
An alien finds them . . .
Boom! A bomb explodes.
A planet destroyed forever.

Brandan John Cassidy (10)
Our Lady Star Of The Sea RCVA Primary School, Peterlee

The Queen Of Light

Space is full of mysteries
From the oily black sky
To the molten, scorching sun
A huge star in the galaxy
At the centre of it all
Like a lamp illuminating the darkness
The Queen of Light.

A great grey sphere of rock and stone
Reflecting the light of the sun
As rocky as a mountain side
It brings on the night and controls the tide
The King of Darkness.

Tom Hilton (11)
Our Lady Star Of The Sea RCVA Primary School, Peterlee

Planet Matune

Beneath the crystal, glittery stars,
Lives a planet as hot as the sun.
Comets orbit the planet.
Agitated aliens waking,
The king alien awakes in his non-gravity palace.
Surrounded by the noisy city,
The deafening factories with their chiming whistles.
The dark and gloomy waves of the sea;
Hitting against the city slopes.
No human would step foot into the planet of Matune,
It would blind them.
The lights shine from one building to another.
All different types of aliens live here –
Big, small, slimy, skinny, furry, spiky, all types!
A completely unique planet,
Miles and miles away.
An unimaginable one!

Katie Leighton (10)
Our Lady Star Of The Sea RCVA Primary School, Peterlee

Nexus

Below the navy blue sky,
Lies an abandoned world,
That world is Nexus.

A city as big as the ocean,
The buildings are as high as the fluffy white clouds,
The people who live there . . . do not look like us.

Red eyes which are as bright as lasers,
Fingernails as sharp as jagged metal,
The people are as tall as lampposts.

The roaring waves clash upon the sloppy mud,
As the sky turns as black as oil,
A world beyond our imagination.

Alan Coles (10)
Our Lady Star Of The Sea RCVA Primary School, Peterlee

The Earth And Moon

Little gems spread across the sky,
A dark blue mist covers space.
A small white ball whizzing around Earth,
The moon orbiting the Earth.

The Earth is big as a hot air balloon,
A big green and blue ball.
It tilts to make seasons,
It orbits the sun.
It also rotates.

The moon comes out at night.
Does it come half or full?
Do you see it at daytime as well?
Sometimes!
It is a big, grey giant,
But small compared to others.

Georgia Roche (10)
Our Lady Star Of The Sea RCVA Primary School, Peterlee

What Am I?

Night-bringer,
Sleepy-timer,
The stars are out,
A big reflection,
Fills the sky.
The one who orbits the Earth.
In day; nowhere to be seen.
Never on the Earth's ground.
Only in the sky at night.
Like a silver round ball in the sky.
Never alone.
Makes you go to sleep at night.
I am the moon.

Quianna Silver (10)
Our Lady Star Of The Sea RCVA Primary School, Peterlee

My Space Poem

Space . . .
Dark mist,
Asteroids,
Stars that light up planets.

Ruco . . .
A planet many galaxies away,
Information I will collect,
From this newly named planet.

I am a stargazer,
A planet explorer,
An asteroid-avoider
In a world of empty planets.

Lucy Rogers (10)
Our Lady Star Of The Sea RCVA Primary School, Peterlee

The City Of Colossus Awakens

The morning comets rush across the sky in a warm welcome.
The palace of Colossus floats up in the dark morning sky.
The prince glares at the illuminating city,
As if it was a million fireworks in one.
The pitch-black sea hurtles in the shores,
Like an arrow hitting a target.
The clouds drift out with the grass green,
Sun peers out into the bright blue sky.
Then finally, the palace brightens up
Like a snow dove in a crow fleet.
Then the city of Colossus awakens.

Rowan Edward Brown (9)
Our Lady Star Of The Sea RCVA Primary School, Peterlee

Space Poem

A never-ending void of darkness,
Illuminated by scorching stars.
Planets all different sizes,
From Jupiter to Mars.
From deep blue to molten red,
All much bigger than cars.

Mercury, Venus, Earth and Mars,
Jupiter, Saturn, Uranus and Neptune.
Black holes then shooting stars,
Comets and of course, the Earth's moon.

Kacper Napora (11)
Our Lady Star Of The Sea RCVA Primary School, Peterlee

Atmosphere

A n ocean-blue sky overthrown by balls of gas,
T he spiralling rays of light are so dazzling they could blind,
M ars rotates rapidly in the distance,
O nly the sound of breathing fills the air,
S o many craters lie on Mercury,
P luto is so small, it is no longer counted as a planet,
H ere comes a blazing asteroid,
E veryone starts to panic,
R unning seems pointless as we aren't going to get far,
E arth no longer exists . . .

Tilly Hudson (11)
Our Lady Star Of The Sea RCVA Primary School, Peterlee

A Bit About Space

Stars shine like glitter,
Creations of gorgeous shapes,
How pretty is space?

The sun shines so bright,
As hot as a fire's heart,
Way bigger than Earth!

Earth is green and blue,
It orbits around the sun,
Earth is where we live!

Jennifer Napora (9)
Our Lady Star Of The Sea RCVA Primary School, Peterlee

The Sun

Hottest star in the sky
Makes you tan and it's so high
If you stare at it, eyes go red
Then it goes to bed.
Then it comes out again
Makes you as red as a teacher's pen.
The sun, the sun, so beautiful . . .
But be careful!

Jay Hutchinson (9)
Our Lady Star Of The Sea RCVA Primary School, Peterlee

Darkness Arises

In the morning fog,
The sky is grey and the planet is calm,
You can hear waves crashing off Planet Mars,
Fire crackling in the sky,
The rocket lands with a bump,
The astronauts leave the safety of their ship,
They smell fear in the air,
What will they find in the darkness?

Courtney Dunnett (10)
Our Lady Star Of The Sea RCVA Primary School, Peterlee

Aliens!

A weird little creature that scatters around.
L ike humans they can talk.
I f you ever see one run inside
E veryone is looking out for where they hide.
N ebulas is where they run.
S oon they are far away and into the sun.

Greg Bell (10)
Our Lady Star Of The Sea RCVA Primary School, Peterlee

Misty Stars

S tars twinkle like little gems.
T he dark object shimmers in the background.
A s evening falls the magic moon appears.
R ockets shooting up, up, up into the night.
S miling happily into the sky . . . What will we see passing by?

Chloe Elisha Mason (10)
Our Lady Star Of The Sea RCVA Primary School, Peterlee

The Wild

Tigers striped and leopards spotted,
Lions hairy and jaguars dotted.
These are the big cats we know and love,
Let's look in the sky and see what's above.
The vultures soar, foraging for their prey,
Owls hunt at night and rest during the day.
Let's take a trip to the sea,
Under the ocean with you and me.
The great white shark hunts all day,
The dolphin and whale play.
Now we've seen the wild and wet,
Let's go home and see our pet.
Cats, dogs and rabbits too,
We love them and they love you.
Now we've seen animals wild and tamed,
All on Earth, rightfully named.

Anna Gelling & Charlotte Parsons (10)
St James' CE Junior School, Barrow-In-Furness

A Night At Space

As I landed up on space,
I could see the moon's shining face.
I saw the sun letting out light,
In the air like a kite.

All around me I find stars,
Seeing long, alien cars.
As I jump on the moon,
It lifts me up like a spoon.

Sometimes I wonder, what is this place?
I want to see a person's face.
Sometimes when I walk on Mars I find,
Beings of a different kind.

Kalvin Knowles (10)
St Paul's CE Junior School, Barrow-In-Furness

Strange Things

I went out through the stars
Passing Neptune, Earth and Mars
Coming across a hidden place
Finding creatures without a trace.

What are they? I thought to myself
A dinosaur, a Minotaur or an alien?
Humongous, terrifying, beastly creatures
Never seen by an eye.

Their skin is so soft
And warm as summer
Friendly, they seem so kind
I thought to myself *what are they?*
Would they hurt me or be kind?

As I went through space
I found many strange things
Where did they come from?
From the land of palaces and kings.

Callum Nesbitt (10)
St Paul's CE Junior School, Barrow-In-Furness

Space

I saw a UFO once
It had its colourful lights
Flashing on and off.
Every time you see the flying object
It shines in the moonlight
And its engine buzzes
Whilst it shoots across the sky like a bullet.
When you look into the spacecraft
You can see a small green creature.
I look into the sky
And see thousands of stars
Glittering like star-shaped lamps.

Dylan Dickson (10)
St Paul's CE Junior School, Barrow-In-Furness

Moving To The Moon

I've finally made it to the moon!
Peering down; down at Earth.
A distant greeny-blue sphere.
Leaving all my troubles behind.

With four frightened, friendly green men.
I take a look to see what's the fuss,
And then they tell me to take a look . . .
A monster! A beast! A four-eyed tyrant!

Here was my chance to be a star.
To save the aliens and save the day
But soon I saw a meteor arriving,
So I told everyone to run as fast as they could!

Flee the beast, run for your lives,
The moon is not what I thought it would be!

Sam Johnston (10)
St Paul's CE Junior School, Barrow-In-Furness

It's Not So Great Upon The Moon

I'd made it to the amazing moon,
On a dismal afternoon,
I bounced around like a loon,
Suddenly falling to my doom,
Down there in the dusty gloom,
I saw a man; his head, a spoon.

It wandered off but I followed the trace,
Leading to a different place!
In that grand, unusual space,
There were green men dancing with lots of grace,
Creatures from a different race,
All quite cute in the face.

My journey's ended oh so soon,
It's not so great upon the moon!

Bobby Steele (11)
St Paul's CE Junior School, Barrow-In-Furness

Space Adventure

As I run through outer space,
Where exactly is this place?
Floating around with lots of grace,
Oh no! I'm in a different race.

Mercury, moon and monstrous Mars,
Crammed next to a shimmer of stars.
Creatures vanishing without a trace,
Not a hint of a body or a face.

'Why me?' I hear me ask myself,
Is this going to be bad for my health?
But then I see a shooting star,
Going faster than a speeding car!

I'm glad I came to this strange place,
Up and up in outer space.
Where all my worries flew away,
Maybe I'll return someday . . .

Darcie Grace Fraser (10)
St Paul's CE Junior School, Barrow-In-Furness

Space Friendship

I saw a small, sweet space girl,
Her skin is green and her name is Pearl.
She lives at the top of ruby-red Mars,
At night she looks at the brightest stars.

For school she goes to the moon
And comes home in the afternoon.
At college she's as cold as ice,
And gets scared when she sees space mice.

She likes to go for a run,
According to her it's very fun.
There's another girl who lives in space,
She is called Grace.

Grace lives to play with her kite,
While the sun is shining bright.
Pearl and Grace are the best of friends,
This is where my story ends.

Kacie Jackson (11)
St Paul's CE Junior School, Barrow-In-Furness

From Moon To Mars

There is a little planet called the moon,
Which houses beings as small as a spoon,
They are looking for a bigger place like Earth or Mars,
Or maybe even across the stars?

They searched for a place to call home,
Where they could place a million domes,
To grow their fluffy, little cones
And rest their brittle bones.

Soon they found the Planet Mars,
With a beautiful view of the stars,
Where they create zooming cars,
And even drinking thinking bars.

Perfectly sleeping alone at night,
Also in the blistering light,
It was such a burning sight,
Nothing could disturb them, the future was bright!

Arthur Mbuli (10)
St Paul's CE Junior School, Barrow-In-Furness

Up In Space

Up in space,
A different race,
One-eyed men,
Their names are Ben.

Daydreaming in my colourful rocket,
Whoosh! I touched a socket!
To the moon; up I go,
Imagining piles of snow.

From the moon I fly to Mars,
Swinging off some metal bars,
Staring at a chained-up beast,
Eyeing me up as its next feast.

In a moon buggy I drive along,
Listening to my favourite song.
Then I start to sing along,
The journey home, it takes too long.

Joe Mallinson (11)
St Paul's CE Junior School, Barrow-In-Furness

Zooming Through Space

Zooming through space on shooting stars,
Passing Earth, the moon and Mars,
I dodged the meteors flying down,
Although I'm still in my dressing gown.

I came across some little green men,
It looked as though they'd made a den,
In a crater on the moon,
I wonder if they will move soon.

They look to me as cold as ice,
Like tiny frozen grains of rice.
Their squeaky voices are so high-pitched,
It sounds like the cackle of a wicked witch.

With dry lagoons and lakes all around,
Tiny bridges lie on the ground.
I do not understand this race,
Up here inside outer space.

Jack Pooley (10)
St Paul's CE Junior School, Barrow-In-Furness

The Man Who Went

A blank sky,
Ready to fly,
Flipping switches to begin the race,
So little time to get into space.

At last the countdown starts,
The thruster's ready; like cooked tarts,
No turning back, forwards into the void,
What can await us? An asteroid?

Finally we're in the air, without a trace,
We're in the air now, where are we going? To a different place!
We've landed on a meteor whizzing around the moon,
Could we go soon?

Back to our rocket,
Through the galaxies to watch the sunset,
No one has gone this far,
Only we have, the sights stick in our mind like hot tar.

Joseph Mbuli (10)
St Paul's CE Junior School, Barrow-In-Furness

A Trip To The Moon

Jupiter, Earth, Pluto too,
Stars and comets next to the moon,
I'm in a rocket circling Mars,
Looking out at the bright, burning stars.

Bang! We landed on the moon,
We've landed next to a spoon,
It might be good with a glass of ice,
But without the ice it's not that nice.

Along came a man,
In a friendly van,
He took me around the moon,
To Mercury, a comet, Saturn and the stars.

It's time to go back to school,
Away from outer space,
The sun has now gone to bed,
The moon shines in its place.

Amelia Taylor (11)
St Paul's CE Junior School, Barrow-In-Furness

Outer Space

Zooming up in outer space,
Discovering a totally different race,
Creatures vanish without a trace,
I think to myself, *what is this place?*

Why is it light,
In the middle of the night?
Is it the stars I see,
Winking at me?

Brrr! It's as cold as ice,
And it's not very nice,
I feel as small as mice,
This has made me think twice.

I want to run,
And be as free as the sun,
Go back to having fun,
When all this space business is done!

Lauren Darby (11)
St Paul's CE Junior School, Barrow-In-Furness

Up In Space

Up in space,
It's a beautiful place,
Some little men having a race,
Some smaller children playing chase.

Soon the race was done,
And Zarg the Zog happily won,
The trophy weighed a ton,
But Zarg said, 'It was fun!'

He went back home,
As dry as a bone,
He got some ice
And ate some rice.

In the middle of the night,
It's a starry lovely sight,
When the stars are orbiting me,
I'm as happy as can be.

Josh Burns (10)
St Paul's CE Junior School, Barrow-In-Furness

Blue, Red, What Colour Is It?

As I dance in outer space,
Wondering who shall I race?
Coming across a funny thing,
Blue, red, what colour is it?

Zooming through the air, racing the little thing,
I feel on top of the moon but it is as tall as a spoon,
We get to the finish line, what a surprise, he won!
What shall I do?

It is as cold as ice,
Why am I here?
What can I play?
Where has that tiny thing gone?

Come out, come out, where are you?
Up, up in the air,
Suddenly I fall in my bed,
Was I dreaming or was it real?

Minnie Sinclair (11)
St Paul's CE Junior School, Barrow-In-Furness

Guess What I Am In Space

Up in this amazing place,
Guess what? I am in space!
Swirling, twirling, beautiful stars,
Ruby-red glittery Mars.

All I wanted to do was lie on the bright warm sun,
Is this possible? Can it be done?
Who thought I would be here on this fine afternoon?
Passing things as lovely as the moon.

As cold as ice I wandered through the night,
Wondering if I'd have to fight,
I needed to find someone nice,
Do I dare or will they take a slice?

I smelt an odd musky scent,
It was coming from a little Green Gent,
'Hey there,' he shouted, 'I am May,
Please can you chat and will you stay?'

Abbie Jean Wheeler (10)
St Paul's CE Junior School, Barrow-In-Furness

Dreaming Of Space

I went walking out one night,
Something gave me such a fright!
As I looked up to the shining stars,
I could see ruby-red Mars.

I levitated off the ground,
My mind was lost but now it's found.
I zoomed off into outer space,
Never again would a human see my face!

As the moon shone on my trace,
I thought *what a wonderful place!*
I saw a nervous little creature,
Staring up with scared, weird features.

How scary, I thought as I looked away,
I'll see it again another day.
I woke up; it's just a dream,
Then I thought of how real it seemed.

Evan Salehi-John (10)
St Paul's CE Junior School, Barrow-In-Furness

YOUNG WRITERS INFORMATION

We hope you have enjoyed reading this book −
and that you will continue to in the coming years.

If you're a young writer who enjoys reading and
creative writing, or the parent of an enthusiastic poet or
story writer, do visit our website
www.youngwriters.co.uk. Here you will find free
competitions, workshops and games, as well as
recommended reads, a poetry glossary and our blog.

If you would like to order further copies of
this book, or any of our other titles give us
a call or visit **www.youngwriters.co.uk.**

Young Writers
Remus House
Coltsfoot Drive
Peterborough
PE2 9BF

(01733) 890066 / 898110
info@youngwriters.co.uk